Mike McGrath

CSS

in
easy steps

second edition

In easy steps is an imprint of In Easy Steps Limited
Southfield Road · Southam
Warwickshire CV47 0FB · United Kingdom
www.ineasysteps.com

2nd Edition

Notice of Liability
Every effort has been made to ensure that this book contains accurate
and current information. However, In Easy Steps Limited and the
author shall not be liable for any loss or damage suffered by readers
as a result of any information contained herein.

Trademarks
All trademarks are acknowledged as belonging to their respective
companies.

In Easy Steps Limited supports The Forest Stewardship Council (FSC),
the leading international forest certification organisation. All our titles
that are printed on Greenpeace approved FSC certified paper carry the
FSC logo.

Mixed Sources
Product group from well-managed
forests and other controlled sources
www.fsc.org Cert no. SGS-COC-005998
© 1996 Forest Stewardship Council

FSC

Printed and bound in the United Kingdom

ISBN 978-1-84078-364-3

Contents

Foreword

The examples in this book have been carefully prepared to demonstrate Cascading Style Sheets. You are encouraged to try out the examples on your own computer to discover the exciting possibilities offered by CSS. The straightforward descriptions should allow you to easily recreate the examples manually or, if you prefer, you can download an archive containing all the source code by following these simple steps:

1 Open your browser and visit our website at **http://www.ineasysteps.com**

2 Navigate to the "Resource Center" and choose the "Downloads" section

3 Find the "From CSS in easy steps, 2nd edition" item in the "Source Code" list, then click on the hyperlink entitled "All Code Examples" to download the ZIP archive

4 Extract the contents of the ZIP archive to any convenient location on your computer – for easy reference these are arranged in sub-folders whose names match each chapter title of this book. The documents are named as described in the book and are located in the appropriate chapter folder of the archive. For example, the **fontfamily.css** style sheet, listed in the fifth chapter, is located in the folder named **5-Formatting text**

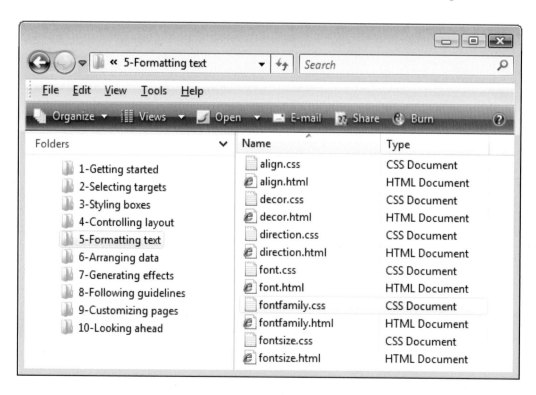

1 Getting started

Welcome to the exciting world of Cascading Style Sheets (CSS). This chapter demonstrates the various ways in which styles can be applied to HTML elements.

Introducing CSS

Cascading Style Sheets (CSS) is a language used to control the presentation of elements within HyperText Markup Language (HTML) documents. Presentation is specified by "styles" that may be assigned "inline" to HTML element **style** attributes, or by "rules" within **<style> </style>** tags in the HTML document's head section, or as rules within separate style sheets. Each style rule selects specified elements then applies specified styles to them.

CSS was created by the World Wide Web Consortium (W3C) to regain control of document markup as HTML grew from the initial few "tags" that merely defined the structural elements of a document – headings, paragraphs, hyperlinks, and lists. Much interest in the Internet arose when the **<img>** tag was introduced, adding the capability to display images alongside text, so websites began to proliferate. Web content authors increasingly began to demand more ways to control how different web page elements should appear, such as bold and italic text – so **<b>** and **<i>** tags were added to HTML. Further tags were also added controlling text color, size, and background color, until it became recognized that the source code of many web pages often contained a great deal of markup for very little actual content.

The W3C offered a solution to regain control of document markup by separating their structural and presentational aspects. HTML tags would continue to control the structure but presentational aspects would now be contolled by "style rules" written in the Cascading Style Sheet (CSS) language. Besides distinguishing between structural and presentational aspects of a document, the CSS solution brings these additional benefits:

- **Easier maintenance** – a single style sheet can control multiple HTML documents, so changing appearance across an entire website is possible by editing just one style sheet

- **Smaller file sizes** – removal of all presentational markup from HTML produces smaller files, which download faster

- **Greater control** – margins, borders, padding, background color, and background images to any HTML element, and the appearance of certain parts of the interface, such as the cursor, can now be specified

Sir Tim Berners Lee, W3C Director and inventor of the World Wide Web

W3C®

The W3C is an international consortium whose members work together to develop web standards. The CSS specifications can be found on their website at **www.w3.org/TR/CSS21**

Understanding the cascade

The term "Cascading" in CSS describes the manner in which style rules can fall from one style sheet to another. The cascade determines which style rule will have precedence over others and be the one applied to the selected HTML element.

There are three basic types of style sheet that can specify style rules to be applied to HTML elements:

 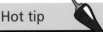
- **Browser (default) style sheet** – browsers employ an intrinsic set of style rules that they apply to all web pages by default. These vary slightly between different browsers but all have common features, such as black text and blue hyperlinks

- **User style sheet** – most browsers allow the user to specify their own appearance preferences, which effectively creates a custom style sheet that overrides the browser's default style sheet

- **Author style sheet** – where the HTML document specifies a style sheet created by the web page author the browser will apply the style rules it contains, overriding both the user style sheet and the default browser style sheet

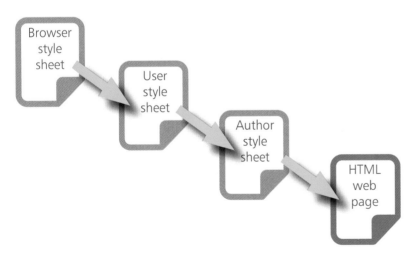

So the cascade means that the browsers will typically apply the style rules in an author style sheet, if present, otherwise it will apply the style rules in a user style sheet, if present, otherwise it will apply the style rules in the browser's style sheet by default.

Creating style rules

In CSS each style rule is comprised of two main parts:

1 **Selector** – specifying which element/s of the HTML document are the target of that rule

2 **Declaration Block** – specifying how properties of the selected target element should be styled

A style rule (or "style rule set") begins with the selector, followed by the declaration block within a pair of curly brackets (braces). The braces contain one or more declarations that each specify a property and a valid value for that property, as in this example:

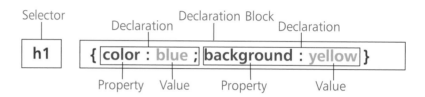

Typically the selector targets (selects) a particular HTML element for styling – such as all **<h1>** heading elements in the document using the style rule set example above.

The declaration block in the example above contains two declarations to determine the foreground and background colors of the selected target elements. The CSS **color** property is assigned a **blue** value – so each **<h1>** heading element will have blue foreground text. Similarly, the CSS **background** property is assigned a **yellow** value – so each **<h1>** heading element will have a yellow background.

Notice how the CSS declaration uses a : colon character to assign a value to a property. Notice also that it requires the declarations to be separated by a ; semi-colon character.

The final declaration in the declaration block does not need to be terminated by a semi-colon. However, some web page authors prefer to habitually terminate all CSS declarations so they need not remember to add a separating semi-colon when adding further declarations to an existing style rule set.

Don't forget

In conformance with the CSS specifications the examples listed throughout this book do not add a semi-colon terminator after the final declaration in a declaration block.

1 When creating a new CSS style rule the author must initially specify a selector to target the HTML element to which the rule will be applied – strictly speaking, the CSS selector is everything that appears before the opening brace of the declaration block

h1

2 Next the declaration block must be created by adding a pair of braces after the selector

h1 {   }

3 Now a declaration can be inserted within the declaration block to assign a value to a property

h1 { color : blue }

4 A second declaration can then be added within the declaration block, separated from the first by a semi-colon

h1 { color : blue ; background : yellow }

5 The style rule set is now complete but can also be applied to another HTML element by extending the selector to become a comma-separated list

h1, h2 { color : blue ; background : yellow }

6 Further style rule sets can then be added below the first style rule set to target other elements

h1, h2   { color : blue ; background : yellow }
p   { color : red }

Hot tip

Whitespace (spaces, tabs, line feeds, and carriage returns) is permitted within style rule sets to allow the author to format the style rules to their own preference. Typically style rule sets with fewer than four declarations are written on a single line, otherwise they are written across multiple lines for clarity.

11

🥾 Creating Style Rules

Heading styled by CSS

Sub-heading styled by CSS

Paragraph styled by CSS

Applying internal style rules

A style sheet is simply a collection of style rule sets to be applied to a HTML document. An internal style sheet can be created by inserting the style rule sets between **<style>** and **</style>** tags in the head section of the HTML document. The opening **<style>** tag should include a **type** attribute assigned a MIME type of "text/css" to describe the style sheet as using the CSS language. Optionally, this tag may also include a **media** attribute assigned a "screen" value to specifically describe the viewing medium as a color computer screen – although this is the default value if the **media** attribute is omitted.

All modern web browsers support CSS but if you wish to hide the internal style sheet from older browsers the style rule sets can be enclosed within **<!--** and **-->** HTML comment tags.

internal.html

1. Create a HTML document containing heading, sub-heading, and paragraph elements

```
<!DOCTYPE HTML PUBLIC "-//W3C//DTD HTML 4.01//EN"
                       "http://www.w3.org/TR/html4/strict.dtd">
<html>
<head>
<meta http-equiv="Content-Type"
                  content="text/html;charset=ISO-8859-1">
<title>Internal style rules</title>
</head>
<body>
<h1>Heading styled by CSS</h1>
<h2>Sub-heading styled by CSS</h2>
<p>Paragraph styled by CSS</p>
</body>
</html>
```

2. In the head section of the document, immediately after the closing **</title>** tag, insert a style element block containing style rule sets for each content element

```
<style type="text/css" media="screen">
<!--
h1      { color : blue ; background : yellow }
h2      { color : white ; background : green }
p       { color : red }
-->
</style>
```

3. Save the HTML file then open it in a web browser to see the styles applied to the content elements

Internal style rules

Heading styled by CSS

Sub-heading styled by CSS

Paragraph styled by CSS

Style rules can also be applied internally to individual HTML elements by assigning "inline" properties and values to the **style** attribute of that element. This will override the rules applicable to the same properties of that element that may have been specified in any other style sheet:

4. Edit the heading elements to reverse the colors specified in the style sheet within the document's head section
```
<h1 style="color : yellow ; background : blue">
                        Heading styled by CSS</h1>
<h2 style="color : green ; background : white">
                        Sub-heading styled by CSS</h2>
```

5. Save the HTML file again then re-open it in a web browser to see the previous styles get overridden

Internal style rules

Heading styled by CSS

Sub-heading styled by CSS

Paragraph styled by CSS

Although described here for completeness there are drawbacks to using internal style rules. Multiple individual inline styles are more difficult to maintain than a single style rule in a style sheet as they would need to be individually altered to affect a style change to a number of elements. An internal style sheet is only applicable to the HTML document in which it is contained, whereas an external style sheet can apply to multiple web pages to consistently style an entire website from a single file.

Don't forget

Internal style sheets should only be used where it is desirable to create a single HTML document for portability – external style sheets, described overleaf, are always preferable.

13

Beware

The use of inline style rules should be avoided at all costs – always place style rules within a style sheet instead.

Linking an external style sheet

An external style sheet is simply a collection of style rule sets listed in a plain text file, such as those created by Windows' Notepad application, then saved with a ".css" file extension. The style sheet can then be linked to HTML documents using a **<link>** tag. This must include a **type** attribute assigned a MIME type of "text/css" to denote using the CSS language, a **rel** attribute assigned a "stylesheet" relationship value, and an **href** attribute assigned the path to the style sheet file. Optionally, this tag may also include a **media** attribute assigned a "screen" value to describe the viewing medium as a color computer screen – although this is the default value if the **media** attribute is omitted.

external-1.html

external-2.html

1 Create two HTML documents containing heading and paragraph elements

```
<!DOCTYPE HTML PUBLIC "-//W3C//DTD HTML 4.01//EN"
                "http://www.w3.org/TR/html4/strict.dtd">
<html>
<head>
<meta http-equiv="Content-Type"
                content="text/html;charset=ISO-8859-1">
<title>External style rules</title>
</head>
<body>
<h1>Heading styled by CSS</h1>
<p>Paragraph styled by CSS</p>
</body>
</html>
```

2 In the head section of each HTML document, immediately after the closing **</title>** tag, insert a link element specifying a style sheet to be used

```
<link type="text/css"
    rel="stylesheet" href="external.css" media="screen">
```

external.css

3 Save the HTML files then open a plain text editor, such as Notepad, and list style rule sets for content elements

```
h2 { color : blue ; background : yellow }
p  { color : red ; background : white }
```

4 Save the CSS file alongside the HTML files, named as "external.css", then open the HTML files in a web browser to see the styles applied to each web page

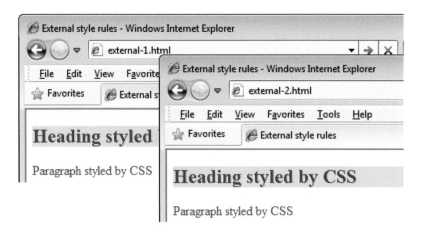

Single line or multi-line comments can be added to CSS style sheets between /* and */ characters. These are ignored by web browsers but are useful to describe aspects of the style sheet.

5. Re-open the style sheet file in a plain text editor and insert a commented title at the very start of the file
/* Master Style Sheet for external-x.html Pages */

6. Now edit the style rule sets to reverse the previous colors
h2 { color : yellow ; background : blue }
p { color : white ; background : red }

7. Save the style sheet file once more then re-open (or refresh) each HTML page in a web browser to see modified style rules applied to both web pages

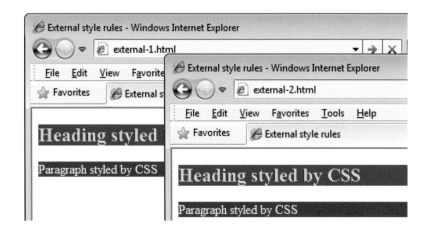

Importing other style sheets

Multiple external style sheets can be used to control different aspects of HTML documents using **@import** directives to specify the path to each CSS file. These must be placed before any other rules in the style sheet and be terminated by a semi-colon.

import.html

1 Create a HTML document containing heading and paragraph elements

```
<!DOCTYPE HTML PUBLIC "-//W3C//DTD HTML 4.01//EN"
                    "http://www.w3.org/TR/html4/strict.dtd">
<html>
<head>
<meta http-equiv="Content-Type"
                content="text/html;charset=ISO-8859-1">
<title>Importing style sheets</title>
</head>
<body>
<h1>Heading styled by CSS</h1>
<h2>Sub-heading styled by CSS</h2>
<p>Paragraph styled by CSS</p>
</body>
</html>
```

2 In the head section of the HTML document, immediately after the closing **</title>** tag, insert a link to a "master" style sheet

```
<link type="text/css"
        rel="stylesheet" href="import.css" media="screen">
```

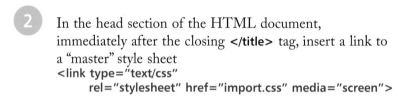

import.css

3 Save the HTML file then open a plain text editor and create the "master" style sheet that simply imports two other style sheets to style the headings and paragraphs within the web page

```
@import "headings.css" ;
@import "paragraphs.css" ;
```

paragraphs.css

4 Save the master style sheet as "import.css" alongside the HTML file then create a style sheet to specify the appearance of paragraphs

```
p { color : blue }
p:first-letter { font-size : xx-large }
```

5 Save the second style sheet as "paragraphs.css" alongside the HTML file then create another style sheet to specify the appearance of headings

h1
{ color : red ;
 font-family : "lucida handwriting", cursive
}

h2 { color : green }

6 Save the third style sheet as "headings.css" alongside the HTML file then open the web page in a browser to see the content elements styled by the style sheets imported via the master style sheet

Beware

Omitting the semi-colon after an @import directive causes the browser to stop reading the style sheet.

Importing style sheets

Heading styled by CSS

Sub-heading styled by CSS

Paragraph styled by CSS

17

7 Edit the "headings.css" style sheet to match all heading colors to the paragraph color then refresh the browser to see the changes

h1
{ color : blue ; font-family : "lucida handwriting", cursive }
h2 { color : blue }

Hot tip

The **@import** directive can be used to hide style sheets from older browsers that do not recognize that instruction.

Importing style sheets

Heading styled by CSS

Sub-heading styled by CSS

Paragraph styled by CSS

Summary

- CSS is a language provided by the W3C to regain control of markup by separating document structure from presentation

- The cascade allows style rules to fall from one style sheet to another and determines which style rule will be applied

- Each style rule comprises of a selector and a declaration block

- Each declaration specifies a property and a value to be applied to that property, separated by a : colon character

- A style rule set contains multiple declarations, each separated from the next by a ; semi-colon character

- The final declaration in a declaration block need not be terminated with a ; semi-colon character

- An internal style sheet is a collection of style rules contained within **<style>** tags in the head section of a HTML document

- Style rules can also be applied inline by assigning properties and values to the **style** attribute of a HTML element

- Inline style rules are difficult to maintain and should be avoided

- External style sheets are recommended to cleanly separate structure and presentation – internal style sheets should only be created in special circumstances

- An external style sheet is a collection of style rule sets listed in a plain text file saved with a **.css** file extension

- An HTML document can link an external style sheet file by adding a **<link>** element in the document's head section

- Each **<link>** element must contain **rel**, **type**, and **href** attributes

- The MIME type of CSS is **text/css**

- All **@import** directives must appear before other rules in a style sheet and must be terminated with a ; semi-colon character

2 Selecting targets

This chapter demonstrates all the different ways in which HTML elements can be selected for styling in CSS.

Selecting by element type

The selector part of a style rule selects elements in a HTML document to be styled according to the values specified in that rule's Declaration Block.

A "type" selector selects all elements in the page that match the selector. Multiple elements can be selected by a type selector that specifies a comma-separated list of element types.

type.html
(fragment)

1 Create a HTML document containing a heading and an unordered list of hyperlinks within a "div" container

```
<div>
<h1>Large Heading</h1>
<ul>
<li><a href="www.google.com">Google</a></li>
<li><a href="www.yahoo.com">Yahoo</a></li>
<li><a href="www.mediafire.com">MediaFire</a></li>
</ul>
</div>
```

type.css

2 Create a linked style sheet with a style rule setting the width of the container element

```
div { width : 20% }
```

3 Add a style rule setting the background color of all hyperlinks

```
a { background : yellow }
```

4 Now add a style rule setting the background color of both the heading and list elements

```
h1, ul { background : fuchsia }
```

5 Save the style sheet file alongside the HTML file then open the web page in a browser to see the elements styled by type selectors

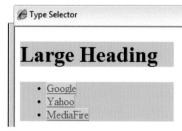

The CSS * universal selector can be used to select elements of all types within a HTML document – as if it was a selector listing all element types as a comma-separated list:

6 Edit the style sheet by adding a style rule with a universal selector to make all text italic
* { font-style : italic }

7 Save the amended style sheet then refresh the browser to see both heading and list text become italic

The * universal selector can also be used to select elements of any type contained within a specified element type:

8 Edit the style sheet by adding a style rule with a universal selector to add a border around all elements within the "div" container
div * { border : 0.2em solid red }

9 Save the amended style sheet then refresh the browser once more to see borders added around the elements

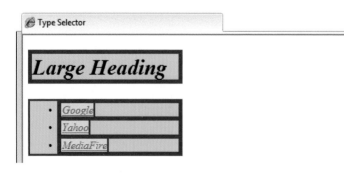

Selecting by class

As an alternative to selecting elements by type, a class selector can select HTML elements that contain a **class** attribute that has been assigned a value matching the selector. The class selector begins with a . period character followed by the class value to match. This is especially useful to apply the style rule across a number of specific elements of different type.

Additionally a class selector can be combined with a type selector to select specific instances of a class. In this case the selector first specifies the element type, followed by a period character and the class value to match:

class.html
(fragment)

class.css

1 Create a HTML document containing a paragraph including two spanned words, in which all elements have a common class value
<p class="frame">You can fool all the people <span class="frame">some</span> of the time, and <span class="frame">some</span> of the people all the time, but you cannot fool all the people all of the time.</p>

2 Create a linked style sheet with a style rule drawing red borders around each element using the class value
.frame { border : 0.2em solid red }

3 Now add a rule overriding the previous one for the paragraph element only, to draw a blue border around the paragraph and set its width
p.frame { border : 0.2em solid blue ; width : 20% }

4 Save the style sheet file alongside the HTML document then open the web page in a browser to see the elements styled by the class selectors

Don't forget

Other paragraphs added to this HTML document would not be styled with this style sheet – unless they too contained a class attribute with the value of "frame".

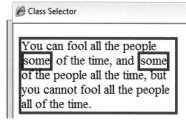

Selecting by identity

Similar to a class selector, an ID selector can select HTML elements that contain an **id** attribute that has been assigned a value matching the selector. The ID selector begins with a **#** hash character followed by the ID value to match. This is mostly useful to apply the style rule to one specific element as each **id** attribute value must be unique within the HTML document.

Optionally an ID selector can be combined with a type selector simply to identify the element type. In this case the selector first specifies the element type, followed by a hash character and the ID value to match:

1. Create a HTML document containing a paragraph including two spanned phrases, in which all elements have a unique ID value
```
<p id="para1">You may only be someone
<span id="span1">in the world</span><br>
but to someone else you may
<span id="span2">be the world</span></p>
```

id.html
(fragment)

2. Create a linked style sheet with style rules painting colored backgrounds behind the text in each span element
```
#span1 { background : yellow }
#span2 { background : lime }
```

id.css

3. Now add a style rule to paint a colored background behind the rest of the paragraph and set its width
```
p#para1 { background : cyan ; width : 30% }
```

4. Save the style sheet file alongside the HTML document then open the web page in a browser to see the elements styled by the ID selectors

ID Selector

You may only be someone in the world
but to someone else you may be the world

Hot tip

If a class selector and an ID selector both attempt to style the same property of one element the ID selector value would be applied as it takes preference.

Selecting descendants

A descendant selector can be used in a style rule to select HTML elements by reference to an outer containing element from which they "descend". For example, a span element within a paragraph element descends from the paragraph element – so a descendant selector of **p span** could be used to select it for styling.

descendant.html
(fragment)

descendant.css

1. Create a HTML document containing an unordered list and an ordered list within a "div" container

```
<div id="menu">
<ul>
<li>Bigger Burger</li>
<li>Buffalo Wings</li>
<li>Deepcrust Pizza</li>
</ul>
<ol>
<li>Cola</li>
<li>Beer</li>
</ol>
</div>
```

2. Create a linked style sheet with style rules to color the items in each list

```
ul li { color : red }
ol li { color : blue }
```

3. Save the style sheet alongside the HTML document then open the web page in a browser to see the list items styled by descendant selectors

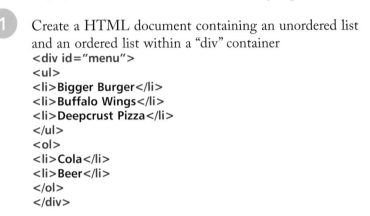

Although it is generally preferable to reference the element from which the target element directly descends it is sometimes useful to simply reference a higher level – say, that from which the containing element descends. This means that the direct containing element is omitted from the selector and the element is selected by reference to the higher level containing element.

4 Edit the style sheet by replacing the previous style rules with a single rule to color the items of both lists in a single color
#menu li { color : green }

5 Save the amended style sheet then refresh the browser window to see the list items styled without reference to their direct containing elements

Don't forget

In this case a descendant selector of **div li** would also select all list items but it is better to reference the **id** value so as not to select list items in other **div** elements.

> *Descendant Selector*
>
> • Bigger Burger
> • Buffalo Wings
> • Deepcrust Pizza
>
> 1. Cola
> 2. Beer

More specific selection can be made, however, by stating each containing element in the line of descent in a descendant selector:

6 Edit the style sheet once more by replacing the previous style rule with two style rules to color the items of both lists in different colors
#menu ul li { color : orange }
#menu ol li { color : purple }

7 Save the newly amended style sheet then refresh the browser window again to see the list items styled by reference to their lines of descent

Hot tip

State the line of descent wherever possible when using descendant selectors to make specific selections.

> *Descendant Selector*
>
> • Bigger Burger
> • Buffalo Wings
> • Deepcrust Pizza
>
> 1. Cola
> 2. Beer

25

Selecting by relationship

Style rules can select elements for styling using the HTML document structure itself. The elements in all HTML documents are arranged in a hierarchical manner descending from the root **<html>** element. The next level contains the **<head>** and **<body>** elements. These each contain nested elements that may, in turn, contain further nested elements... and so on to complete the hierarchy. The hierarchy of a simple HTML document could resemble this tree view:

Hot tip

This tree view represents the HTML document in the example opposite.

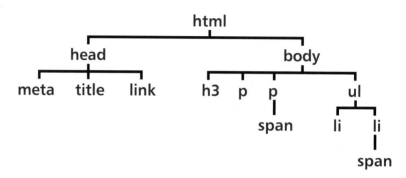

The hierachy between a containing element and a nested element on the next hierarchical level can be described as a parent - child relationship. So **<html>** is the parent of the **<head>** and **<body>** elements, who are themselves children of the **<html>** element. Similarly, the **<head>** element is the parent of the **<meta>**, **<title>**, and **<link>** child elements, and the **<h3>**, **<p>**, and **<ul>** elements are all children of the **<body>** parent element.

A style rule child selector can select specific child elements by stating the parent name followed by the **>** right angled-bracket character then the child name. For example, a child selector of **p > span** selects all span elements within paragraph elements.

The child selector can even state the hierarchy completely back to the root element if preferred, such as **html > body > p > span**.

Another selector that selects elements by relationship is the adjacent sibling selector. This selects the first sibling element after a specified element – by stating the specified element name followed by the **+** plus character then the sibling name. For example, an adjacent sibling selector of **h3 + p** selects any **<p>** paragraph element that immediately follows a **<h3>** heading element where both have the same parent.

Don't forget

As with people, all elements are a parent or a child, or in many cases they are both.

26

1 Create a HTML document containing a heading, two paragraphs, a list, and including two spanned phrases

```
<body>
<h3>Heading : Child</h3>
<p>Paragraph : Child</p>
<p>Paragraph : Child
             <span>Span : Grandchild</span></p>
<ul>
<li>List Item : Grandchild</li>
<li>List Item : Grandchild
             <span>Span : Great Grandchild</span></li>
</ul>
</body>
```

relative.html
(fragment)

2 Create a linked style sheet with a style rule to select the first sibling immediately following the heading

```
h3 + p { background :  yellow }
```

relative.css

3 Next add a style rule to select the span child of the paragraph element

```
p > span { background : lime }
```

4 Now add style rules to select in turn each descendant element in the list by describing its hierarchy

```
body > ul { background : fuchsia }
body > ul > li { background : aqua }
body > ul > li > span { background : orange }
```

5 Save the style sheet alongside the HTML document then open the web page in a browser to see the elements styled by sibling and child selectors

> **Hot tip**
>
> The text in this example describes each element's relationship to the **\<body>** element.

27

Child and Sibling Selectors

Heading : Child

Paragraph : Child

Paragraph : Child Span : Grandchild

- List Item : Grandchild
- List Item : Grandchild Span : Great Grandchild

Selecting by attribute

Style rules can select HTML elements for styling by matching an attribute that the element contains. The selector in this case specifies the attribute name within square brackets. For example, a selector of *[src] would select all elements containing a **src** attribute – irrespective of their assigned values.

Additionally, the attribute selector can specify multiple attributes to select only those elements containing all the specified attributes. For example, a selector of *[src][alt] would select all elements containing both **src** and **alt** attributes – irrespective of their assigned values.

More specific selection is possible by stating an assigned value to match in the selector. For example, a selector of *[lang="en"] would select all elements containing a **lang** attribute that have an assigned value of **"en"**.

attribute.html
(fragment)

1. Create a HTML document with five anchor elements
   <div><a id="top">Anchor</a></div> <hr>

   <div><a href="http://www.google.com">Web Hyperlink</a></div> <hr>

   <div><a href="http://www.google.com" title="Google">Web Hyperlink + Title</a></div> <hr>

   <div><a href="#top" title="Top of the Page" >Page Hyperlink</a></div> <hr>

   <div><a id="bottom">Anchor</a></div>

attribute.css

2. Create a linked style sheet with a style rule to paint the background of all anchors containing an **id** attribute
   a[id] { background : orange }

3. Add a style rule next to color the text in all hyperlinks containing a **href** attribute
   a[href] { color : red }

4. Next add a style rule to paint the background of all hyperlinks containing both a **href** attribute and a **title** attribute
   a[href][title] { background : yellow }

5 Now add a style rule to draw a border around all hyperlinks that have a href attribute assigned a #top value
a[href="#top"] { border : 0.2em solid blue }

6 Save the style sheet alongside the HTML document then open the web page in a browser to see styles applied to elements selected by their attributes

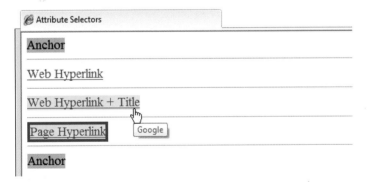

Don't forget

The * "wild card" universal selector selects all elements that match.

Selecting partial attributes

Style rules can select HTML elements for styling by matching partial attribute values. This allows the selector to target an element based upon the presence of any single word in an attribute containing a space-separated list of words. Typically, this technique might be used to match one of the words assigned to the **class** attribute of a HTML element.

The syntax to match a single word in an attribute list adds a ~ tilde character to the selector, such as *[class~="word"] – to match all elements that have a **class** attribute assigned a "word" value.

Additionally, a style rule selector can select a HTML element for styling by matching the beginning of an assigned attribute value. Typically, this technique might be used to match values assigned to HTML lang attribute values or a series of images.

The syntax to match the beginning of a value assigned to a HTML attribute adds a | pipe character to the selector, such as *[lang|="es"] – to match all elements that have a **lang** attribute assigned a value beginning with "es".

30

partial.html
(fragment)

1 Create a HTML document containing an ordered list in which all elements have a **class** attribute
```
<ol>
<li class="reptile">Alligator</li>
<li class="animal">Race Horse</li>
<li class="animal">Domestic Cat</li>
<li class="fish">Barracuda</li>
<li class="toy animal">Teddy Bear</li>
</ol>
```

2 Add an unordered list in which all elements have a **lang** attribute
```
<ul>
<li lang="en-us">Hello America</li>
<li lang="es">Hola España</li>
<li lang="es-mx">Hola México</li>
</ul>
```

3 Add a paragraph containing two sets of images

```
<p>
<img src="ring-1.gif" alt="Ring Image">
        <img src="box-1.gif" alt="Box Image">
<img src="ring-2.gif" alt="Ring Image" >
                    <img src="box-2.gif" alt="Box Image" >
<img src="ring-3.gif" alt="Ring Image" >
                    <img src="box-3.gif" alt="Box Image" >
</p>
```

partial.css

4 Save the HTML file, then create a style sheet with a rule to select elements in the ordered list according to the value assigned to their **class** attributes

```
*[class~="animal"] { background : lime }
```

5 Now add a rule to select elements in the unordered list according to the beginning of the value assigned to their **lang** attributes

```
*[lang|="es"] { color : red ; background : yellow }
```

6 Next add rules to select **img** elements according to the beginning of the value assigned to their **src** attributes

```
*[src|="ring"] { background : fuchsia }
*[src|="box"] { background : aqua }
```

7 Save the style sheet alongside the HTML document then open the web page in a browser to see styles applied by selecting partial attribute values

Partial Selectors

1. Alligator
2. Race Horse
3. Domestic Cat
4. Barracuda
5. Teddy Bear

• Hello America
• Hola España
• Hola México

Evaluating importance

After the cascade considers the origin of style rules, as described on page 9, the browser then evaluates their "weight" to determine which rules have most weight and should, therefore, be applied.

Weight can be added to any style rule by including a CSS **!important** declaration to elevate its status. For example, the rule **h2 { color : red !important }** takes precedence over another rule of **h2 { color : blue }** and the red color will be applied.

Although regular Author style sheet rules take precedence over regular User and Browser style sheet rules, an **!important** User style sheet rule overrides an **!important** Author style sheet rule. So the cascade sorts style sheet rules by origin and weight into this order, from most weight to least weight:

(1) **!important** User style sheet rules

(2) **!important** Author style sheet rules

(3) regular Author style sheet rules

(4) regular User style sheet rules

(5) regular Browser style sheet rules

Where more than one style rule of equal weight targets properties of the same element the browser then evaluates their importance by examining their selector's "specificity" – to consider how specifically each one targets the element. The specificity evaluation process awards points for each selector component, which get stored in four "registers" for later comparison against the specificity value of conflicting selectors. So the specificity value can be expressed as a comma separated list – in which 0,0,0,0 is a zero specificity value. The selector component points are awarded like this:

- For each element and pseudo-element in the selector add 0,0,0,1

- For each **class** attribute value, attribute selection, or pseudo-class in the selector add 0,0,1,0

- For each **id** attribute in the selector add 0,1,0,0

- For inline **style** attribute declarations add 1,0,0,0

Don't forget

The * wildcard selector has a zero specificity value of 0,0,0,0.

32

Hot tip

More details about pseudo-elements and pseudo-classes can be found within the Reference Section, on pages 184-186.

In comparing specifity values the registers are examined individually, reading from left to right, until a difference is found. The style rule with the highest value in that register is then applied. For example, in comparing specificity values of 0,1,0,0 and 0,0,0,1 a difference occurs in the second register.

1 Create a HTML document containing three headings
```
<h2>Element style</h2>
<h2 id="heading-2">Identity style</h2>
<h2 class="headers">Class style</h2>
```

importance.html (fragment)

2 Next create a linked style sheet containing rules that both target the heading elements' color property
```
h2 { color : yellow !important }
h2 { color : black }
```

importance.css

3 Now add rules that each target the heading elements' background property in different ways
```
h2 { background : aqua }              /* 0,0,0,1 */
body h2 { background : blue }         /* 0,0,0,2 */

#heading-2 { background : maroon }    /* 0,1,0,0 */
h2#heading-2 { background : red }     /* 0,1,0,1 */

h2.headers { background : olive }     /* 0,0,1,1 */
body h2.headers { background : green } /* 0,0,1,2 */
```

4 Save the style sheet alongside the HTML document then open the web page in a browser to see the elements styled

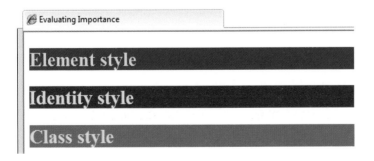

34

Summary

- A type selector selects all elements of the specified type and multiple elements can be specified as a comma-separated list

- The * universal selector can be used to select all elements

- The . class selector selects all elements containing a **class** attribute that has been assigned a specified value

- The **#** ID selector selects all elements containing an **id** attribute that has been assigned a specified value

- A descendant selector specifies both an element type and a type of element from which it descends, separated by space

- A **>** child selector specifies both the parent element type and the child element type from which it descends, to select the child elements

- The **+** adjacent sibling selector specifies an element type and the element type of an adjacent sibling to be selected

- The [] attribute selector specifies an element type followed by the name of an attribute within square brackets, to select all specified elements containing that attribute

- Optionally, an [] attribute selector can also specify an attribute value within the brackets to select only elements of the specified type that contain a specified attribute of that value

- An attribute selector can match a single word in an attribute list using the ~= syntax in the square brackets

- An attribute selector can match the beginning of an attribute value using the |= syntax in the square brackets

- A style rule can be made to override another by adding an **!important** declaration to elevate its status

- After the cascade arranges style rule importance by origin, it then considers their weight and specificity to determine which rules should be applied

3 Styling boxes

This chapter demonstrates how to style the boxes that contain web page content.

Recognizing content boxes

Content on a web page is displayed in a number of invisible rectangular boxes that are generated by the browser. These content boxes may be either "block level" or "inline".

Block-level content boxes normally have line breaks before and after the box, such as paragraph, heading, and "div" elements.

Inline content boxes, on the other hand, do not add line breaks but are simply created within lines of text, such as span, emphasis, and hyperlink elements.

Each block-level content box comprises a core content area surrounded by optional areas for padding, border, and margins:

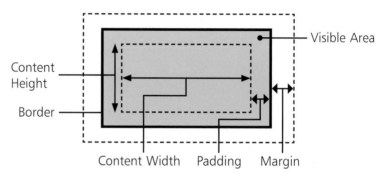

Style rules can specify values for the padding, border, and margin properties to control the appearance of content boxes. These all apply to block-level boxes but some properties, such as width and height, do not apply to inline boxes. Additionally, the margin and padding properties of inline boxes only apply to either side of the content – not the areas above and below the content.

When the padding, border, and margin properties all have a zero width the content box will be the same size as the content area, determined by the dimensions of the content.

Any padding, border, and margin areas that have a non-zero width are added outside the content area, so the content size remains the same but the box size increases.

The padding property extends the area around the content and inherits the background color of the content area. The border property extends the area around the content and any padding. The margin property extends the area around the content, any padding, and any border, with a transparent background.

Hot tip

Block-level content boxes are by default stacked on the page, one below another, whereas inline content boxes appear within a block-level box, one behind another.

1. Create a HTML document with four simple paragraphs, three with assigned class attribute values
```
<p>Content Box</p>
<p class="pad">Content Box - Padded</p>
<p class="pad bdr">Content Box - Padded + Border</p>
<p class="pad bdr mgn">Content Box -
                 Padded + Border + Margin</p>
```

box.html
(fragment)

2. Save the HTML document then create a linked style sheet with a style rule that sets the width and background color of the core content area
```
p { background : yellow ; width : 20em }
```

box.css

3. Next add a style rule to add some padding
```
p.pad { padding : 1em }
```

4. Now add a style rule to add a border
```
p.bdr { border : 0.5em red solid }
```

5. Finally add a style rule to add a margin
```
p.mgn { margin : 2em }
```

6. Save the style sheet alongside the HTML document then open the web page in a browser to see the content boxes with added padding, borders, and margin

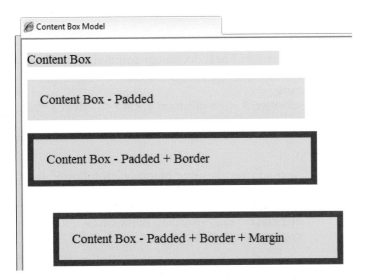

Changing display formats

A web page relies upon the creation of block-level content boxes, to determine its general layout, and the creation of inline content boxes within the blocks to determine its precise layout.

This places great emphasis on whether an element is considered block-level or inline to determine the display format. Generally the default display format for each element will be the most appropriate. For example, it's generally desirable to display list items on individual lines in a block-level list.

The display format of an element can also be explicitly determined by a style rule that assigns the **block** or **inline** keywords to that element's **display** property. This means that content can be displayed in a different format without changing the HTML tags. For example, list items can be displayed on a single line with a **display : inline** declaration.

Where two block-level elements follow each other the first can be made to be displayed as if it was an inline box within the beginning of the second block by assigning its **display** property the **run-in** keyword. For example, applying a run-in style rule to a heading that is followed by a paragraph will display the heading apparently within the start of the paragraph block.

Additionally an inline content-box can have its **display** property assigned an **inline-block** value to allow it to be displayed somewhat like a block-level content box. The inline-block still appears inline, as usual, but unlike regular inline content boxes its **width** and **height** properties can be assigned values to control its size.

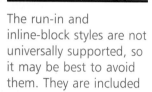

Beware

The run-in and inline-block styles are not universally supported, so it may be best to avoid them. They are included here for completeness.

display.html
(fragment)

1 Create a HTML document containing two unordered list blocks, with one assigned a class attribute value
```
<ul>
<li>Item 1 </li><li>Item 2 </li><li>Item 3 </li></ul>
<ul class="line">
<li>Item 1 </li><li>Item 2 </li><li>Item 3 </li></ul>
```

2 Next add two heading blocks, each followed by a paragraph block, with one assigned a class attribute value
```
<h2>Heading Block</h2><p>Paragraph Block</p>
<h2 class="run">Heading Block</h2>
<p>Paragraph Block</p>
```

3 Next add a paragraph block containing three inline hyperlink content boxes

```
<p>
<a href="1.html">Page 1</a>
<a href="2.html">Page 2</a>
<a href="3.html">Page 3</a>
</p>
```

4 Save the HTML document then create a linked style sheet with a rule to display one list's items inline

ul.line li { display : inline ; background : aqua }

display.css

5 Add another style rule to run one heading block into the following paragraph block

h2.run { display : run-in ; background : yellow }

6 Then add a style rule to change the inline hyperlink content boxes into inline blocks so their height and width can be adjusted

p a { display : inline-block ;
width : 4em ; height : 4em ; background : lime }

7 Save the style sheet alongside the HTML document then open the web page in a browser to see the content displayed in default and non-default display formats

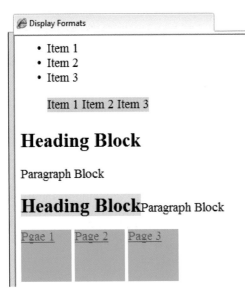

Don't forget

Assigning a non-default display type to an element only changes the way it gets displayed – in the document tree inline elements are always descendants of block-level elements.

Sizing the content area

When assigning any non-zero value to a property the declaration must include a two-letter unit name to specify which unit of measurement to apply. The CSS specification provides the following unit names representing real world measurement:

Unit	Description	Example
in (inches)	American standard unit of length measurement	**div { width : 1in }**
cm (centimeters)	Metric unit of length where 2.54 centimeters is equivalent to 1 inch	**div { height : 2.54cm }**
mm (millimeters)	Metric unit of length (one tenth of one centimeter) where 25.4 millimeters is equivalent to 1 inch	**div { height : 25.4mm }**
pt (points)	Typographical unit of font height where 72 points is equivalent to 1 inch	**div { font-size : 72pt }**
pc (picas)	Typographical unit of font height where 6 picas is equivalent to 1 inch	**div { font-size : 6pc }**

The CSS specification also provides the following unit names representing relative values according to the viewing device:

Unit	Description	Example
em (font size)	Abstract typographical unit of font size where 1em is equivalent to the height of a given font	**div { font-size : 14pt }** (1em = 14pt)
ex (font size)	Abstract typographical unit of font size where 1ex is equivalent to the height of lowercase "x" in a font (often 50% of 1em)	**div { font-size : 14pt }** (1ex = 7pt)
px (pixels)	Abstract unit representing the dots on a computer monitor where there are 1024 pixels on each line when the monitor resolution is 1024x768	**div { height : 100px }**

1 Create a HTML document containing 4 "div" elements
```
<div id="absolute">3in x ½in</div>
<div id="container">400px x 200px
  <div id="percent">50% x 50%</div>
  <div id="relative">20em x 2em</div>
</div>
```

size.html (fragment)

2 Save the HTML document then create a linked style sheet with a rule to size an element by absolute units
```
div#absolute { width : 3in ; height : 0.5in ;
                    background : red ; color : yellow }
```

size.css

3 Next add a rule to size an element by monitor resolution
```
div#container { width : 400px ; height : 200px ;
                    background : blue ; color : aqua }
```

4 Now add a rule to size an element by percentage
```
div#percent { width : 50% ; height : 50% ;
                    background : green ; color : yellow }
```

5 Then add a rule to size an element relative to font height
```
div#relative { width : 20em ; height : 2em ;
                    background : yellow ; color : blue }
```

6 Save the style sheet alongside the HTML document then open the web page in a browser to see the element sizes

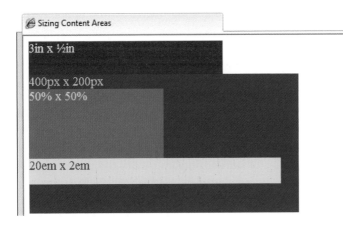

41

Hot tip

It is often considered good practice to use **em** units wherever possible for maximum flexibility.

Controlling borders

Each content box can have a border comprising **border-width**, **border-color**, and **border-style** properties. A value can be specified to each of these individual properties to apply a uniform border to all four sides of the content box, or a space-separated list of values can be specified to apply different borders to each side:

- When two values are listed the first is applied to the top and bottom borders

- When three values are listed the first is applied to the top border, the second is applied to the left and right borders, and the third is applied to the bottom border

- When four values are listed they are applied clockwise to the top, right, bottom, and left borders

The default **border-width** value is **medium** (a computed value), and the default **border-color** value is inherited from the element's **color** property, but the default **border-style** is **none**. This means that the border will not be visible until a value is assigned – possible **border-style** values are **solid, double, dotted, dashed, groove, ridge, inset, outset, hidden,** and **none**.

Rather than creating separate style rules for the **border-width, border-color**, and **border-style** properties it is simpler to use the CSS shorthand technique that specifies a value for each of these three properties to a **border** property as a space separated list. This uniformly styles each side of the content box with a border of the specified width, color, and style. For example, a style rule declaration of **border : 0.5in red dotted** would apply a half-inch wide red dotted border to all four sides of the content box.

If it is desirable to have different styles the borders on each side of a content box can be individually styled by creating rules for the element's **border-top, border-right, border-bottom,** and **border-left** properties. The CSS shorthand technique can also be used with these properties to specify a width, color, and style for the individual side as a space separated list. For example, a style rule declaration of **border-bottom : 0.5in red dotted** would apply a half-inch wide red dotted border to just the bottom side of the content box.

Hot tip

The **outset** border style can be used to create the appearance of a raised button – and the **inset** border style can be used to create the appearance of a depressed button.

1. Create a HTML document containing four paragraphs
```
<p id="p1">Solid - Inherit - Medium</p>
<p id="p2">Top: Dotted - Orange - 0.2em
          <br>Bottom: Dashed - Green - 0.2em</p>
<p id="p3">Ridge Double - Blue - 1em</p>
<p id="p4">Outset - Yellow - 1em</p>
```

border.html (fragment)

2. Save the HTML document then create a linked style sheet with a rule to add a border that inherits a color
```
#p1 { color : red ; border : solid }
```

border.css

3. Next add a rule with shorthand declarations to create a border above and below the content area only
```
#p2 { border-top : 0.5em orange dotted ;
      border-bottom : 0.5em green dashed }
```

4. Now add a rule creating a border from separate properties
```
#p3 { border-style : ridge double ;
      border-width : 1em ;
      border-color : blue }
```

5. Then add a rule creating a border on all four sides using the recommended CSS shorthand technique
```
#p4 { border : 1em yellow outset }
```

6. Save the style sheet alongside the HTML document then open the web page in a browser to see the borders

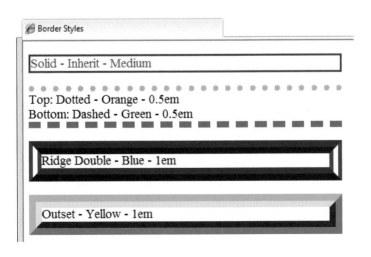

Border Styles

Solid - Inherit - Medium

Top: Dotted - Orange - 0.5em
Bottom: Dashed - Green - 0.5em

Ridge Double - Blue - 1em

Outset - Yellow - 1em

Hot tip

Notice how the browser miters the borders diagonally where they meet – this offers some creative possibilities.

43

Adding padding

Each content box can have "padding" space added around the core content area by a style rule assigning a value to the **padding** property. A single value can be specified to apply a uniform padding width to all four sides of the content area, or a space-separated list of values can be specified to apply different padding widths to each side:

- When two values are listed the first is applied to the top and bottom sides and the second is applied to the left and right

- When three values are listed the first is applied to the top side, the second is applied to the left and right sides, and the third is applied to the bottom side

- When four values are listed they are applied clockwise to the top, right, bottom, and left sides

The padding area surrounds the core content area and extends to the outer edges of the border area if a border is specified – right up to the beginning of the margin area. The element's background fills the core content area and the padding area, so that any specified background color gets automatically applied to both the core content area and the padding area.

The **padding** property can be specified as a unit value or as a percentage value. When a percentage is specified the padding width is calculated using the width and height of the containing element – and the padding area size will be adjusted if the size of the containing element gets changed.

Typically a padding area is specified when adding a border to an element to increase the space between the content and the border.

If it is desirable to have different padding widths on each side of a content box the padding can be individually styled by creating rules for the element's **padding-top, padding-right, padding-bottom,** and **padding-left** properties. For example, style rule declarations of **padding-top : 0.5in ; padding-bottom : 0.5in** would apply a half-inch padding area to top and bottom sides. Alternatively, the same result can be achieved using the CSS shorthand with a declaration of **padding : 0.5in 0 0.5in 0.**

44

1 Create a HTML document containing three paragraphs that each include a span element and are separated by horizontal ruled lines

```
<p>Horizontally
        <span id="pad-h">Padded</span> Content.</p>
<hr>
<p>Vertically
        <span id="pad-v">Padded</span> Content.</p>
<hr>
<p>Horizontally and Vertically
        <span id="pad-hv">Padded</span> Content.</p>
```

padding.html
(fragment)

2 Save the HTML document then create a linked style sheet with rules to color the paragraph and span elements

```
p { background : aqua }
span { background : yellow ; border : 0.3em red dashed }
```

padding.css

3 Next add a style rule to add padding to the left and right sides of the first span content box

```
span#pad-h { padding : 0 3em 0 3em }
```

4 Now add a style rule to add padding to the top and bottom sides of the second span content box

```
span#pad-v { padding : 1em 0 1em 0 }
```

5 Then add a style rule to add uniform padding to all sides of the third span element

```
span#pad-hv { padding : 1em }
```

6 Save the style sheet alongside the HTML file then open the web page in a browser to see the added padding

Don't forget

Notice how the background color fills the content area and padding area – extending up to the outer edge of the border area.

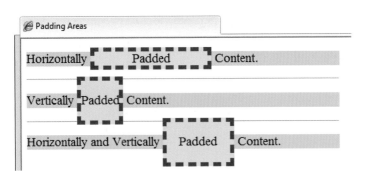

Setting margins

Each content box can have outer "margin" space added around the entire content, padding, and border areas by a style rule assigning a value to the **margin** property. A single value can be specified to apply a uniform margin width to all four sides of the content box, or a space-separated list of values can be specified to apply different margin widths to each side:

The ability to automatically compute the margin size is essential for centering content – as described on page 56.

Hot tip

- When two values are listed the first is applied to the top and bottom sides and the second is applied to the left and right

- When three values are listed the first is applied to the top side, the second is applied to the left and right sides, and the third is applied to the bottom side

- When four values are listed they are applied clockwise to the top, right, bottom, and left sides

The **margin** property has a default value of zero but in reality the browser applies its own intrinsic default values to allow spacing between elements. For example, heading elements always allow a margin area before a following paragraph element.

The **margin** property can be specified as a unit value, or as a percentage value, or with the **auto** keyword to have the browser compute a suitable margin.

Margins do not inherit any background and are always transparent – they merely separate elements by a specified distance.

Hot tip

The margin width for each side can always be set using the CSS **margin** shorthand by setting sides requiring no margin to zero – always use the shorthand.

If it is desirable to have different margin widths on each side of a content box the margin can be individually styled by creating rules for the element's **margin-top, margin-right, margin-bottom,** and **margin-left** properties. For example, style rule declarations of **margin-top : 0.5in ; margin-bottom : 0.5in** would apply a half-inch margin area to top and bottom sides. Alternatively, the same result can be achieved using the CSS shorthand with a declaration of **margin : 0.5in 0 0.5in 0**.

1 Create a HTML document containing three "div" elements that each contain a heading element and a paragraph element

```
<div><h2>Heading - Default Margin</h2>
<p>Paragraph - Default Margin</p></div>
<div><h2 class="zero">Heading - No Margin</h2>
<p class="zero">Paragraph - No Margin</p></div>
<div><h2 class="left">Heading - Left Margin</h2>
<p class="left">Paragraph - Left Margin</p></div>
```

margin.html
(fragment)

2 Save the HTML document then create a linked style sheet with rules to color the elements

```
div { border : 1px solid black }
h2 { background : lime }
p { background : fuchsia }
```

margin.css

3 Next add a style rule to remove all margins from the second heading and paragraph element content boxes

```
.zero { margin : 0 }
```

4 Now add a style rule to add a left margin only to the third heading and paragraph element content boxes

```
.left { margin : 0 0 0 0.5in }
```

5 Save the style sheet alongside the HTML file then open the web page in a browser to see the margin styles

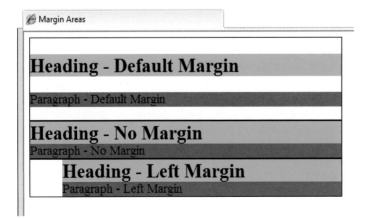

Painting colors

The listed examples so far in this book have employed color keywords to represent the 17 CSS "standard" colors as below:

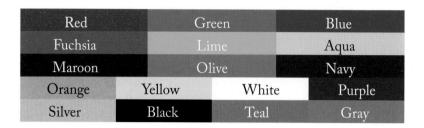

Red	Green	Blue
Fuchsia	Lime	Aqua
Maroon	Olive	Navy
Orange	Yellow	White	Purple
Silver	Black	Teal	Gray

While the standard named colors are convenient to use they provide only a limited choice. Fortunately CSS allows authors to create their own custom colors.

Each color can be defined by the amount of red, green, and blue that needs to be mixed together to form that particular color. For example, the standard olive color comprises 50% red, 50% green and 0% blue. This can be expressed in RGB notation form as **rgb(50%, 50%, 0%)** for assignment to a CSS property like this:

h1 { color : rgb(50%, 50%, 0%) }   /* Olive headings */

Specifying different amounts of red, green, and blue, in this way the author can assign to a property any custom color desired.

As an alternative to specifying each color component as a percentage the author may choose an integer value in the range 0-255 for each component. In this format the RGB notation for the standard olive color looks like this:

h1 { color : rgb(128, 128, 0) }   /* Olive headings */

A second alternative to specifying each color component as a percentage allows the author to choose a hexadecimal value in the range 00-FF for each component. In this format the assignment for the standard olive color looks like this:

h1 { color : #808000 }   /* Olive headings */

The table opposite lists the ways in which each standard color can be assigned to a property using these various methods.

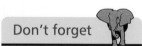

Don't forget

Web browsers often recognize many more color names (often up to 140) but those shown here are the standard color names defined in the CSS specifications.

Color	Percentage	Integer	Hex
Black	rgb(0%,0%,0%)	rgb(0,0,0)	#000000
Red	rgb(100%,0%,0%)	rgb(255,0,0)	#FF0000
Orange	rgb(100%,65%,0%)	rgb(255,165,0)	#FFA500
Yellow	rgb(100%,100%,0%)	rgb(255,255,0)	#FFFF00
Fuchsia	rgb(100%,0%,100%)	rgb(255,0,255)	#FF00FF
Lime	rgb(0%,100%,0%)	rgb(0,255,0)	#00FF00
Aqua	rgb(0%,100%,100%)	rgb(0,255,255)	#00FFFF
Blue	rgb(0%,0%,100%)	rgb(0,0,255)	#0000FF
White	rgb(100%,100%,100%)	rgb(255,255,255)	#FFFFFF
Maroon	rgb(50%,0%,0%)	rgb(128,0,0)	#800000
Olive	rgb(50%,50%,0%)	rgb(128,128,0)	#808000
Purple	rgb(50%,0%,50%)	rgb(128,0,128)	#800080
Green	rgb(0%,50%,0%)	rgb(0,128,0)	#008000
Teal	rgb(0%,50%,50%)	rgb(0,128,128)	#008080
Navy	rgb(0%,0%,50%)	rgb(0,0,128)	#000080
Gray	rgb(50%,50%,50%)	rgb(128,128,128)	#808080
Silver	rgb(75%,75%,75%)	rgb(192,192,192)	#C0C0C0

Hexadecimal color values comprising three pairs of matching digits can alternatively be expressed using CSS shorthand notation that represents each pair of digits as a single digit. For example, the hexadecimal value for the standard red color is **#FF0000** but can be specified in shorthand as **#F00**. Similarly black **#000000** can be written as **#000** and white **#FFFFFF** as **#FFF**.

The author is free to choose which color notation method to use according to their preference. Declarations in the style rules below show how each method might be used to specify a custom color:

```
h1 { color : rgb( 85%, 15%, 0% ) }    /* A custom red */
h2 { color : rgb( 0, 192, 12 ) }      /* A custom green */
h3 { color : #042BDF }                /* A custom blue */
h4 { color : #DE2 }         /* A custom yellow (#DDEE22) */
```

Hot tip

In hex notation, you can specify "web safe" consistent colors by using only digits that are multiples of 3 for the red, green and blue.

Repeating backgrounds

Each content box can have a background color specified by assigning a valid color value to its **background** property. Alternatively an image can be specified for the background by assigning a **url(*filename*)** value, where *filename* is the path to an image file – this should not be enclosed within quotes.

The **background-color** and **background-image** properties can be used to specify both a background image and background color. Any specified background image will normally be positioned at the top left corner of the content box. The default behavior of the browser's **background-repeat** property is set to **repeat** so the image will be tiled, row-by-row, across the content box.

The tiling behavior can be modified by assigning different values to the **background-repeat** property where values of **repeat-x** restricts the tiling pattern to one horizontal row and **repeat-y** restricts the tiling pattern to one vertical column. Tiling can also be prevented by assigning a **no-repeat** value so that a single copy of the image appears at the top left corner of the content box.

Background images are placed on a layer above the background's color layer so specifying an image with transparent areas will allow the background color to shine through.

Using CSS shorthand the color, image, and repeat values can simply be assigned as a space-separated list to the **background** property. These may appear in any order and default values are assumed for any value not specified in the list. For example, the **background-repeat** property is assumed to have a **repeat** value unless another value is specified.

Hot tip

Use the **background** property shorthand rather than the various individual properties – to keep the style sheet more concise.

background.html
(fragment)

① Create a HTML document with four paragraphs that each contain a span element
`<p><span>`**Repeat - Default**`</span></p>`

`<p id="x"><span>`**Repeat-X**`</span></p>`

`<p id="y"><span>`**Repeat-Y**`</span></p>`

`<p id="no"><span>`**No Repeat**`</span></p>`

2 Save the HTML document then create a linked style sheet containing a rule to style the span elements
span { background : yellow ; margin : 0 0 0 10em }

background.css

3 Next add a style rule to specify the background color, background image, and height of each paragraph
p {   background : url(tile.gif) fuchsia repeat ;
height : 3.5em }

4 Now add a style rule to modify the tiling behavior of the second paragraph to one row
p#x { background-repeat : repeat-x }

5 Then add a style rule to modify the tiling behavior of the third paragraph to one column
p#y { background-repeat : repeat-y }

tile.gif – the red areas are transparent.

6 Finally add a style rule to modify the tiling behavior of the fourth paragraph to just one copy of the image
p#no { background-repeat : no-repeat }

7 Save the style sheet alongside the HTML document then open the web page in a browser to see the background color and image applied

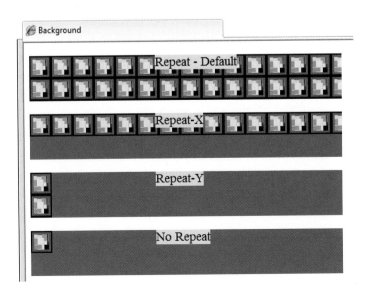

Don't forget

The **repeat** value could be omitted from the rule in step 3 – as that is the default value.

Positioning backgrounds

A background image is, by default, positioned at the top left corner of the content box but this can be modified by specifying a different value to the **background-position** property. This can accept keywords of either **left, center, right, top,** and **bottom**. Two of these keywords may be used to specify the position, separated by a space, such as **top center**. Alternatively just one of these keywords can be specified and the second value will be assumed to be **center**.

The **background-position** property can also be assigned percentage values to specify the position with greater precision, taken from the dimensions of the containing element. The keywords have the equivalent to these percentages:

X-Axis			Y-Axis
			top **(0%)**
left **(0%)**	**center** **(50%)**	**right** **(100%)**	**center** **(50%)**
			bottom **(100%)**

When specifying position with percentages the first value sets the X-axis position and the second value sets the Y-axis position. If only one percentage is specified the second is assumed to be 50%. Interestingly, when computing the background image position the browser first identifies a point within the image at the specified coordinates, then places that point at the same coordinates within the content box. For example, with values of **50% 50%** the browser first identifies a point at the exact center of the image then places that point at the exact center of the content box.

The **background-attachment** property has a **scroll** value by default so the background image scrolls with the page but a style rule can specify a **fixed** value so it remains at specified coordinates relative to the viewport when the page gets scrolled.

Both **background-position** and **background-attachment** property values can be specified to the CSS **background** property, along with the **background-color, background-image,** and **background-repeat** values described on the previous page.

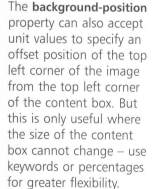

Hot tip

The **background-position** property can also accept unit values to specify an offset position of the top left corner of the image from the top left corner of the content box. But this is only useful where the size of the content box cannot change – use keywords or percentages for greater flexibility.

1 Create a HTML document with three paragraphs that each contain a span element
```
<p><span>Top Left - Default</span></p>
<p id="p1"><span>Bottom Left</span></p>
<p id="p2"><span>20% 50%</span></p>
```

position.html
(fragment)

2 Save the HTML document then create a linked style sheet containing rules to style the spans and paragraphs
```
span { background : yellow ; margin : 0 0 0 10em }
p { background : url(tile.gif) fuchsia no-repeat ;
                                       height : 3.5em }
```

position.css

3 Now add rules to position paragraph background images using keywords and percentages
```
p#p1 { background-position : bottom left }
p#p2 { background-position : 20% 50% }
```

4 Finally add a rule to fix a background image in the page that will remain positioned when the page gets scrolled
```
body { background : url(tile.gif) no-repeat
                             bottom right fixed }
```

5 Save the style sheet alongside the HTML document then open the web page in a browser to see the positioned background images

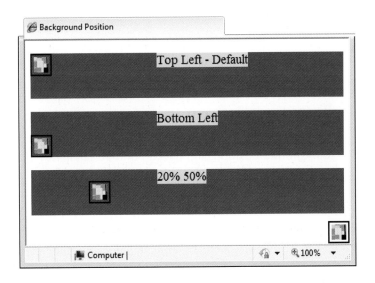

Summary

- Block-level content boxes add line breaks before and after the box – but inline content boxes appear within lines of text

- The core content area of a content box can be surrounded by **padding**, **border**, and **margin** areas

- A content box's **display** property can be used to change its display format from block-level to inline, and vice versa

- Content box dimensions can be specified to **width** and **height** properties as absolute values of **in, cm, mm, pt**, and **pc** units, or as relative values of **em, ex**, and **px** measurements

- The **border** property can specify the individual **border-width**, **border-color**, and **border-style** properties using CSS shorthand

- Border styles may be **solid, double, dotted, dashed, groove, ridge, inset, outset, hidden** or **none**

- The **padding** property can specify the individual **padding-top**, **padding-right, padding-bottom**, and **padding-left** properties using CSS shorthand

- The **margin** property can specify the individual **margin-top**, **margin-right, margin-bottom**, and **margin-left** properties using CSS shorthand

- Colors can be specified using the standard color keywords, or as a three-part **rgb()** value with percentage or numerical parts, or as a single hexadecimal value

- The **background** property can specify the individual **background-color, background-image, background-repeat, background-position**, and **background-attachment** properties using CSS shorthand

- Background images can be specified as a **url()** value in which the path to the image file is stated within the parentheses

4 Controlling layout

This chapter demonstrates how to position content boxes to control page layout.

Centering content boxes

One of the basic requirements in displaying document components is the ability to horizontally center blocks of content – in the same way provided by the old HTML **<center>** tag.

In CSS the ability to horizontally center block-level elements is provided by the **margin** property and the **auto** keyword.

When the **auto** keyword is specified to an element's **margin** property the browser first calculates the distance to the left and right of that element, up to the boundaries of its containing element, then divides the total in half to compute the value of each side margin. For example, applying a **margin : auto** to a "div" element of 80px width, that is contained within an outer element of 200px width, the browser divides the total difference of 120px in half then applies 60px wide margins to each side of the div element – so it gets positioned centrally within the containing element.

Notice that **margin : auto** does not center vertically but merely sets the top and bottom margins to zero, so there are no margin areas above or below the element block.

It is important to recognize that **margin : auto** centers block-level content boxes and should not be confused with **text-align : center** that can be used to center content within inline content boxes.

center.html
(fragment)

1 Create a HTML document with a "div" element containing two further elements
```
<div>Default Position
  <div class="inner">Default Position</div>
  <div class="inner center">Centered Block</div>
</div>
```

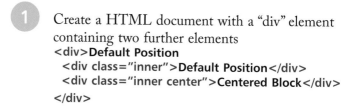

2 Now add another "div" element containing three further elements
```
<div class="center">Centered Block
<div class="inner">Default Position</div>
<div class="center inner">Centered Block</div>
<div class="center inner center-text">
                Centered Block + Centered Content</div>
</div>
```

…cont'd

3 Save the HTML document then create a linked style sheet containing a style rule to specify default width, margin, and colors for each element
**div { width : 20em ; margin : 0 0 2em 0 ;
border : 0.1em solid black ; background : orange }**

center.css

4 Next add a style rule over-writing the previous rule for inner elements
div.inner { margin : 0 ; width : 10em ; background : yellow }

5 Now add a rule to center inner elements
div.center { margin : auto ; background : aqua }

6 Finally add a style rule to center content within an inner element
div.center-text { text-align : center ; background : lime }

7 Save the style sheet alongside the HTML document then open the web page in a browser to see the centered content boxes and centered content

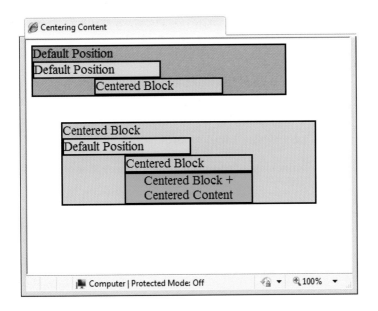

Hot tip

When the browser window gets resized the second outer "div" element gets automatically repositioned to become horizontally centered again.

Positioning boxes absolutely

When laying out the element content boxes of a web page the CSS **position** property has a default value of **static** – representing the normal flow positioning scheme. Assigning a different value to an element's **position** property allows that element to be removed from the normal flow so it can be positioned independently.

Alternatives to the default **static** value can be specified using the **absolute, relative,** and **fixed** keywords to specify an alternative positioning scheme to that of the normal flow layout.

The **absolute, relative,** and **fixed** positioning schemes each use one or more of the CSS "offset" properties **top, right, bottom,** and **left,** to define their position.

When the position property is specified as **absolute** the positioning scheme places the element at the specified offset distance from the boundaries of its containing element. For example, a "div" element with top and left values of 100px will be positioned 100px below and to the right of its container boundaries.

absolute.html
(fragment)

1. Create a HTML document with four "div" elements that each contain an inner div element

```
<div class="top-left large">Top:0 Left:0
 <div class="btm-right small">Bottom:0 Right:0</div>
</div>

<div class="top-right large">Top:0 Right:0
 <div class="btm-left small">Bottom:0 Left:0</div>
</div>

<div class="btm-left large">
                         <br><br><br>Bottom:0 Left:0
 <div class="top-right small">Top:0 Right:0</div>
</div>

<div class="btm-right large">
                         <br><br><br>Bottom:0 Right:0
 <div class="top-left small">Top:0 Left:0</div>
</div>
```

2 Save the HTML document then create a linked style sheet with rules to set the absolute size of the elements

div.large { width : 200px ; height : 90px ;
border : 1px solid black }

div.small { width : 80px ; height : 50px ;
border : 1px solid black }

absolute.css

3 Now add style rules to set the absolute position of each element

div.top-left { position : absolute ; top : 0px ; left : 0px ;
background : lime }

div.top-right { position : absolute ; top : 0px ; right : 0px ;
background : aqua }

div.btm-left { position : absolute ;
bottom : 0px ; left : 0px ; background : yellow }

div.btm-right { position : absolute ;
bottom : 0px ; right : 0px ; background : orange }

4 Save the style sheet alongside the HTML document then open the web page in a browser to see the content boxes positioned at absolute coordinates

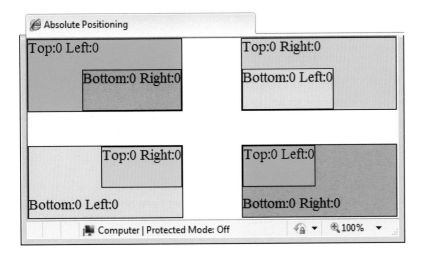

Stacking content boxes

Changing from the **static** default positioning scheme, by assigning the **absolute** value to the **position** property, allows elements to overlap – stacking one above the other in the same order they are listed in the HTML code.

The stacking order can be explicitly specified however in CSS by assigning an integer value to the **z-index** property of each element. The element with the highest value appears uppermost, then beneath that appears the element with the next highest value, and so on.

So the **absolute** positioning scheme allows element position to be precisely controlled in three dimensions using XYZ coordinates – along the X axis with the **left** and **right** offset properties, along the Y axis using the **top** and **bottom** offset properties, and along the Z axis using the **z-index** stacking order property.

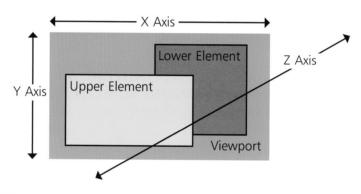

stack.html
(fragment)

1. Create a HTML document containing four "div" elements to be positioned overlapping
   `<div id="pale-gray"> </div>`

   `<div id="lite-gray"> </div>`

   `<div id="dark-gray"> </div>`

   `<div id="text-box">Text content here on the top of the element stack - lower offset elements create a drop shadow effect</div>`

stack.css

2 Save the HTML document then create a linked style sheet containing a rule to set the size of all elements
div { width : 400px ; height : 50px }

3 Next add a style rule to position the uppermost element
**div#text-box {   position : absolute ;
                    top : 20px ; left : 20px ;
                    background : yellow ; z-index : 4 }**

4 Now add a rule to position the next element below
**div#dark-gray { position : absolute ;
                    top : 24px ; left : 24px ;
                    background : #666 ; z-index : 3 }**

5 Then add a rule to position an element further below
**div#lite-gray {   position : absolute ;
                    top : 28px ; left : 28px ;
                    background : #999 ; z-index : 2 }**

6 Finally add a rule to position the lowest element
**div#pale-gray { position : absolute ;
                    top : 32px ; left : 32px ;
                    background : #CCC ; z-index : 1 }**

7 Save the style sheet alongside the HTML document then open the web page in a browser to see the elements positioned in all three dimensions

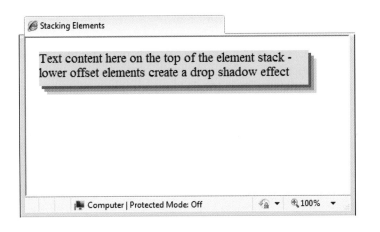

Hot tip

A smaller offset creates a more convincing drop shadow effect – a large offset is used here to illustrate the contribution of each element.

Positioning boxes relatively

In contrast to the **absolute** positioning scheme, which entirely removes an element from the normal flow layout, a **relative** positioning scheme adjusts the position of an element relative to the position it would originally occupy in the normal flow layout.

Changing from the default **static** positioning scheme, by assigning the **relative** value to the CSS **position** property, allows elements to be repositioned from their normal flow layout position using the offset properties **top**, **right**, **bottom** and **left**.

For example, specifying a **top** value of -18px moves the selected element up and specifying a **left** value of 100px moves it to the right – but crucially the space occupied by its original layout position is preserved. Applying these relative position values to a span element within a paragraph has this effect:

> a repositioned span element
> There is   on this line - it pays no
> heed to other paragraph content for it is an inline content box

Notice how the original content is shifted from its normal flow layout position into a newly-created content box positioned at the specified distance relative to its original position. This relative position will be maintained, even when the position of the outer containing element is changed.

So while **absolute** positioning may typically control the position of the outer element the **relative** positioning scheme is often useful to control the position of nested inner elements.

62

relative.html
(fragment)

1. Create a HTML document containing four nested "div" elements to be positioned overlapping

```
<div id="pale-gray">
 <div id="lite-gray">
  <div id="dark-gray">
   <div id="text-box">Text content here on the innermost
        element - outer offset elements create a drop
        shadow effect</div>
  </div>
 </div>
</div>
```

2 Save the HTML document then create a linked style sheet containing a rule to set the size and color of the outermost containing element

div#pale-gray { width : 400px ; height : 50px ;
background : #CCC ; margin : 20px }

relative.css

3 Next add a style rule to position the first nested element relative to the outermost containing element

div#lite-gray { position : relative ; left : -4px ; top : -4px ;
height : 100% ; background : #999 }

4 Now add a style rule to position the second nested element relative to the first nested element

div#dark-gray { position : relative ; left : -4px ; top : -4px ;
height : 100% ; background : #666 }

5 Finally add a style rule to position the innermost nested element relative to the second nested element

div#text-box { position : relative ; left : -4px ; top : -4px ;
height : 100% ; background : lime }

6 Save the style sheet alongside the HTML document then open the web page in a browser to see the nested elements positioned relative to their containing elements

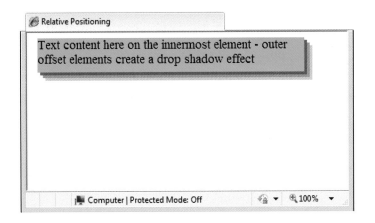

Hot tip

The **margin** property is only set on the outer element simply to move the content away from the edge of the window.

63

Fixing constant positions

A **fixed** positioning scheme, like the **absolute** positioning scheme, completely removes the selected element's content box from the normal flow layout. But unlike **absolute** positioning, where offset values relate to the boundaries of the containing element, in **fixed** positioning the offset values relate to the viewport – the position is relative to the browser window, not to any part of the document.

Usefully element positions can be fixed to emulate a frame-style interface where some frames remain at a constant position regardless of how the regular page is scrolled. For example, a banner header frame can be fixed at the top of the page so it remains constantly visible even when the page is scrolled:

fixed.html
(fragment)

fixed.css

1 Create a HTML document containing a heading element and a paragraph with a tall image to scroll
```
<h1>Header</h1>
<p>
<img src="ruler.png" width="71" height="521" alt="Ruler">
</p>
```

2 Save the HTML document then create a linked style sheet with a rule to fix the heading element to the top of the browser window and above other page content
```
h1 { position : fixed ; top : 0 ; left : 0 ; margin : 0 ;
                background : lime ; width : 100% ; z-index : 2 }
```

3 Now add a style rule to position the paragraph below the heading element
```
p { position : absolute ; top : 100px ; z-index : 1 }
```

4 Save the style sheet alongside the HTML document then open the web page in a browser to see the elements positioned by the style rules

5 Now scroll the browser window to see the heading remain in place while the paragraph content slides beneath it

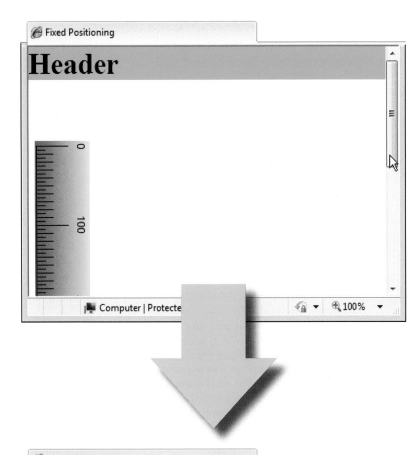

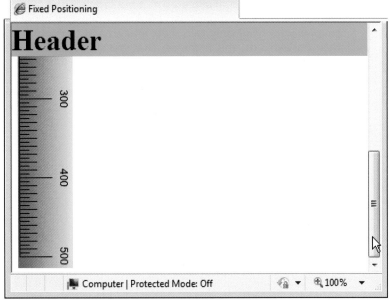

Hot tip

Fixed positioning is sometimes used to display an identity logo that remains visible at a constant position regardless of where the page is scrolled.

Floating content boxes

The CSS **float** property allows a content box to be positioned at the side boundary of its containing element – using the **left** or **right** keywords to specify the preferred side.

Unusually, floated content boxes are not truly removed from the normal flow layout but are repositioned within it. Space is not preserved at their original position but is, instead, filled with surrounding content which flows around the floated content box. Typically this feature is used to flow text around images that have been floated to the side of a containing paragraph element.

It is, however, possible to explicitly prevent text flowing alongside a floated content box using the CSS **clear** property – specifying **left**, **right**, or **both** keywords to determine which side must be clear, so that text will begin below the floated content box.

float.html
(fragment)

1 Create a HTML document containing three paragraphs and two images

```
<p>Massive acceleration - the forbidden fruit! It's easy to avoid such unlawful <img src="viper-1.jpg" width="150" height="128" alt="Viper Front"> activities in a normal vehicle. But there is an evil serpent; a Viper that tempts you to take a bite out of the asphalt. With a tasty 500-hp V10 powering a mere 3,300-lb roadster, the Dodge Viper SRT-10 tricks you into playing music with the loud pedal.</p>

<p>This car is too excessive, too epic for most people to use on a daily basis. <img src="viper-2.jpg" width="155" height="115" alt="Viper Rear">But for otherwise nice couples who need only two seats and a need to explore their darkest sins, this is the car that will shame those who come up against them.</p>

<p class="clear">If you can afford to... Buy one. You need it. You'll like it.</p>
```

float.css

2 Save the HTML document then create a linked style sheet with a rule to color all paragraph backgrounds
```
p { background : yellow }
```

3 Now add a style rule to float the first image to the right side of its containing paragraph element and add a border
```
img[src="viper-1.jpg"] { float : right ;
                         border : 3px dashed red }
```

4 Next add a style rule to float the second image to the left side of its containing paragraph element and add a border
img[src="viper-2.jpg"] { float : left ;
                                    border : 3px dashed blue }

5 Save the style sheet alongside the HTML document then open the web page in a browser to see the floated images

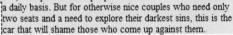

Floating Content Boxes

Massive acceleration - the forbidden fruit! It's easy to avoid such unlawful activities in a normal vehicle. But there is an evil serpent; a Viper that tempts you to take a bite out of the asphalt. With a tasty 500-hp V10 powering a mere 3,300-lb roadster, the Dodge Viper SRT-10 tricks you into playing music with the loud pedal.

This car is too excessive, too epic for most people to use on a daily basis. But for otherwise nice couples who need only two seats and a need to explore their darkest sins, this is the car that will shame those who come up against them.

If you can afford to... Buy one. You need it. You'll like it.

6 Edit the style sheet to add a rule that prevents the final paragraph flowing alongside the second floated image
p.clear { clear : left }

7 Save the style sheet once more then refresh the browser window to see the final paragraph now appear below the second image

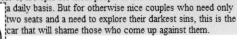

Floating Content Boxes

Massive acceleration - the forbidden fruit! It's easy to avoid such unlawful activities in a normal vehicle. But there is an evil serpent; a Viper that tempts you to take a bite out of the asphalt. With a tasty 500-hp V10 powering a mere 3,300-lb roadster, the Dodge Viper SRT-10 tricks you into playing music with the loud pedal.

This car is too excessive, too epic for most people to use on a daily basis. But for otherwise nice couples who need only two seats and a need to explore their darkest sins, this is the car that will shame those who come up against them.

If you can afford to... Buy one. You need it. You'll like it.

Clipping & handling overflow

Although CSS provides many controls to specify the precise size and position of content boxes there is no guarantee that their content will fit neatly within their boundaries in all circumstances. For example, consider the effect of increasing the font size of text content that fits snugly within a block-level content box – the text will then "overflow" outside the box boundaries.

Overflowing content is generally **visible** by default, but the CSS **overflow** property can specify alternative handling behaviors using the **hidden** or **scroll** keywords.

Conversely, the content within absolutely positioned block-level content boxes can be cropped using the **clip** property – the rectangular section to remain visible being identified by the coordinates of its corner points. In CSS these coordinates are assigned to the **clip** property as a comma-separated list within the parentheses of the special **rect()** keyword, always in the order of top-left, top-right, bottom-right, bottom-left.

overflow.html
(fragment)

1. Create a HTML document with six "div" elements that each contain the same image
```
<div class = "crop auto-clip">
                  <img src = "p.png" alt="Blocks"></div>

<div class = "crop blok-clip">
                  <img src = "p.png" alt="Blocks" ></div>

<div class = "crop line-clip">
                  <img src = "p.png" alt="Blocks" ></div>

<div class = "spill show-overflow">
                  <img src = "p.png" alt="Blocks" ></div>

<div class = "spill hide-overflow">
                  <img src = "p.png" alt="Blocks" ></div>

<div class = "spill keep-overflow">
                  <img src = "p.png" alt="Blocks" ></div>
```

overflow.css

2. Save the HTML document then create a linked style sheet with rules that specify the absolute position and size of each div element
```
div.crop{ position : absolute ; top : 20px ;
                      width : 100px ; height : 100px }
div.spill { position : absolute ; top : 150px ;
                      width : 75px ; height : 75px }
```

3 Add a style rule that allows the first image to be automatically cropped to the full image size
div.auto-clip { left : 20px ; clip : auto }

4 Next add style rules that crop the visible part of the second and third image to reveal only those parts of the image within specified coordinates
div.blok-clip
{ left : 140px ; clip : rect(25px, 100px, 100px, 25px) }

div.line-clip
{ left : 260px ; clip : rect(25px, 100px, 50px, 0px) }

5 Now add a style rule that allows those parts of the fourth image that overflow the content box to be visible
div.show-overflow { left : 20px ; overflow : visible }

6 Add a style rule to hide those parts of the fifth image that overflow the content box
div.hide-overflow { left : 140px ; overflow : hidden }

7 Finally add a style rule to hide those parts of the sixth image that overflow the content box and provide scroll bars so hidden parts can be viewed
div.keep-overflow { left : 260px ; overflow : scroll }

8 Save the style sheet alongside the HTML document then open the web page in a browser to see the cropped images and compare how the overflow is handled

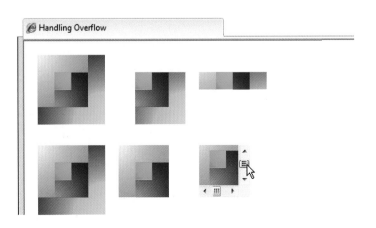

Handling Overflow

Don't forget

Currently only rectangular areas can be clipped, but future specifications may allow other shapes to be clipped.

Hot tip

The ability to toggle content visibility, between visible and hidden, presents exciting dynamic possibilities – see chapter 7 for more details and examples.

Constructing columns

Traditionally web page authors have used HTML tables to control how page content is laid out by creating a borderless grid of cells into which components of the page are placed. This method works well enough for general layout but lacks the precise control offered by CSS. For example, the **absolute** positioning scheme allows components to be easily positioned with pinpoint accuracy but this could not be easily achieved using tables. Thus CSS provides a superior layout method so web page authors are now discouraged from using HTML tables for this purpose.

Moving to page layout with CSS invariably raises questions of how best to control the page content. The following example suggests one way to create a common page layout featuring a header and footer plus three content columns:

columns.html
(fragment)

1   Create a HTML document containing "div" elements for header and content panels, all wrapped in an outer container element that is followed by a footer element
```
<div id="wrapper">
```

```
<div id="hdr">Header Panel<br>
<img src="box.gif" width="250" height="25" alt="Box">
</div>
```

```
<div id="nav">Navigation Panel
<ul><li>Link<li>Link</ul></div>
```

```
<div id="ads">Supplement Panel<br>
<img src="box.gif" width="75" height="100" alt="Box">
</div>
```

```
<div id="txt">Content Panel<br>
<img src="box.gif" width="150" height="200" alt="Box">
</div>
```

```
</div>
```

```
<div id="ftr">Footer Panel</div>
```

columns.css

2   Save the HTML document then create a linked style sheet with a rule to remove all margins and padding, and to center all content
```
* { margin : 0 ; padding : 0 ; text-align : center }
```

3 Add a rule to ensure the page is the entire window height
html, body { height : 100% }

4 Now add a rule to have the container element use the entire window area – except for a bottom margin area where the footer will appear
#wrapper { min-height : 100% ; height : auto !important ; height : 100% ; margin : 0 auto -30px }

5 Next add style rules to set the header and footer heights and background color
#hdr { height : 60px ; background : aqua }
#ftr { height : 30px ; background : aqua }

6 Finally add rules to position and color the three columns
#nav { float : left ; width : 100px ; background : yellow }
#ads { float : right ; width : 100px ; background : fuchsia }
#txt { margin : 0 100px ; background : lime }

7 Save the style sheet alongside the HTML document then open the web page in a browser to see the page layout

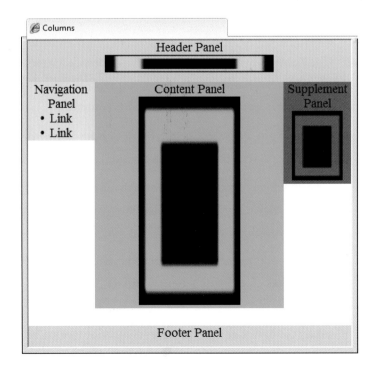

Summary

- A **margin : auto** rule horizontally centers block-level content boxes, acting much like the old HTML **<center>** tag

- A **text-align : center** rule horizontally centers text within a content box

- The **absolute, relative,** and **fixed** positioning schemes use the **top, right, bottom,** and **left** properties to specify position

- A **position : absolute** rule removes an element from the normal flow layout and positions it at a specified distance from the boundaries of its containing element

- The stacking order of overlapping elements can be specified by assigning integer values to their **z-index** property

- A **position : relative** rule moves an element from the position it would occupy in the normal flow layout and preserves the space it would have occupied

- A **position : fixed** rule removes an element from the normal flow layout and positions it at a specified distance from the boundaries of the viewport

- The **float** property accepts **left, right,** or **both** keywords to reposition an element within the normal flow layout and fill the space it would have occupied with content

- The **clear** property accepts **left, right,** or **both** keywords to explicitly prevent text flowing alongside a floated content box

- Overflowing content is **visible** by default but the **overflow** property can accept **hidden** or **scroll** keywords to specify alternative behavior

- The **clip** property accepts the **rect()** keyword that specifies the coordinates of a clipping area within its parentheses

- Web page authors are now discouraged from using HTML tables for layout as CSS provides a superior layout method

5 Formatting text

This chapter demonstrates how to suggest specific font styles for text content.

Suggesting a font

A CSS style rule can suggest a specific font to be used by the browser for the display of text content in a selected element by specifying the font name to its **font-family** property. The browser will use the specified font if it is available on the user's system – otherwise it will display the text using its default font.

The default font may not be the best choice for the author's purpose so CSS additionally allows the **font-family** property to suggest a generic font family from those in the table below:

Font Family	Description	Example
serif	Proportional fonts where characters have different widths to suit their size, and with serif decorations at the end of the character strokes	**Times New Roman**
sans-serif	Proportional fonts without serif decorations	**Arial**
monospace	Non-proportional fonts where characters are of fixed width, similar to type-written text	**Courier**
cursive	Fonts that attempt to emulate human hand-written text	**Comic Sans**
fantasy	Decorative fonts with highly graphic appearance	**Castellar**

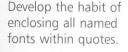
Hot tip

Develop the habit of enclosing all named fonts within quotes.

The browser will first try to apply the named font but in the event that it is unavailable will select a font from those available that most closely matches the charcteristics of the generic preference. In this way the appearance of the text should at least approximate the author's intention, even without specific font-matching.

In a style rule **font-family** declaration the preferred font name should appear before the generic font family preference separated by a comma. Multiple named fonts can be specified as a comma-separated list – all before the generic font family preference. Font names that include spaces must be enclosed within quotes or they will not be recognized by the browser.

1. Create a HTML document containing a paragraph with several spanned sections of text

```
<p>The <span class="serif">City of New York</span>
was introduced to professional football on the same day
that the city was introduced to the
<span class="fantasy">New York Giants</span>.
It was a clear sunny
<span class="mono">October afternoon in 1925</span>
when the Giants took the field to play against the
<span class="cursive">Frankford Yellow Jackets</span>.
</p>
```

fontfamily.html
(fragment)

2. Save the HTML document then create a linked style sheet containing a rule suggesting a default font for the entire paragraph

```
p { font-family : "Arial Narrow", sans-serif }
```

fontfamily.css

3. Next add style rules suggesting fonts for the spanned text

```
span.serif { font-family : "Times New Roman", serif }
span.fantasy { font-family : "Castellar", fantasy }
span.mono { font-family : "Courier", monospace }
span.cursive { font-family :
            "Lucida Handwriting", "Comic Sans", cursive }
```

4. Save the style sheet alongside the HTML document then open the web page in a browser to see the sections of text appear in the named fonts or generic family fonts

---

Font Family

The City of New York was introduced to professional football on the same day that the city was introduced to the NEW YORK GIANTS. It was a clear sunny October afternoon in 1925 when the Giants took the field to play against the *Frankford Yellow Jackets*.

Don't forget

It is good practice to specify a generic font family preference in every **font-family** declaration.

75

Specifying font size

CSS provides a number of ways to specify the size of text in a style rule declaration by assigning values to the **font-size** property. The most obvious is as an absolute size using any of the absolute units listed on page 40. For example, as a **12pt** size like this:

#text-1 { font-size : 12pt }

Additionally CSS provides the keywords **xx-small**, **x-small**, **small**, **medium**, **large**, **x-large**, and **xx-large** to specify an absolute size.

Keyword	Equivalent
xx-large	24pt
x-large	17pt
large	13.5pt
medium	12pt
small	10.5pt
x-small	7.5pt
xx-small	7pt

Here the **medium** size is determined by the browser's default font size then the rest are computed relative to that size.

Where the default size is equivalent to **12pt** the computed values might look something like those in the table on the left.

So a style rule might specify a font size one scale higher than the default font size like this:

#text-2 { font-size : large }

Declarations may also specify a font size one scale higher or lower using the **larger** and **smaller** keywords like this:

#text-3 { font-size : larger }

Alternatively font size can be specified as a relative size using any of the relative units listed on page 40. For example, double the inherited size (or default size if none is inherited) like this:

#text-4 { font-size : 2em }

Similarly, font size can be specified as a relative size stated as a percentage. For example, as five times the inherited or default size with a style rule declaration like this:

#text-5 { font-size : 500% }

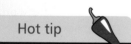

Hot tip

Use relative values rather than absolute values to specify font sizes for maximum flexibility.

1. Create a HTML document containing a paragraph with several spanned sections of text

```
<p>This 12pt high text can become
<span class = "lg">larger</span> or
<span class = "sm">smaller</span> <br>It can get
<span class = "xxl">extremely large</span> or
<span class = "xxs">extremely small</span> <br>
and it may even grow to be
<span class = "huge">huge</span>
</p>
```

fontsize.html
(fragment)

2. Save the HTML document then create a linked style sheet containing a rule specifying a default font size for the entire paragraph

```
p { font-size : 12pt }
```

fontsize.css

3. Next add style rules specifying font sizes for the spanned sections of text

```
span.lg { font-size : larger }
span.sm { font-size : smaller }
span.xxl { font-size : xx-large }
span.xxs.{ font-size : xx-small }
span.huge { font-size : 500% }
```

4. Save the style sheet alongside the HTML document then open the web page in a browser to see the sections of text appear in the specified font sizes

Font Size

This 12pt high text can become larger or smaller

It can get extremely large or extremely small

and it may even grow to be huge

Adjusting font weight

The thickness or "weight" of text can be easily adjusted using the CSS **font-weight** property and the **bold** and **normal** keywords.

Specifying a **bold** value to a selected element's **font-weight** property causes normally weighted text to appear in a heavier font and specifying a **normal** value causes heavily weighted text to appear in a lighter font. In actuality the browser uses two different fonts to achieve this effect – for **normal** text it uses a regularly weighted font (for example "Verdana") but it switches to the heavier weighted variant of that font if one is available (such as "Verdana Bold") for **bold** text.

As an alternative to the bold and normal keywords a font weight can be specified as a numeric value from 100-900, by hundreds. A **font-weight** value of **400** is equivalent to **normal** weight and a value of **700** is equivalent to **bold** weight.

It is intended that this numeric weighting system should allow for font variants other than the **normal** and **bold** ones to be allotted to intermediate values. For example, a font lighter than the **normal** font (say, "Verdana Light") could equate to the weight value **300**. Similarly, a font heavier than the **bold** font (say, "Verdana Bold Black") could equate to the numeric weight value **800**.

In practice, however, the numeric system typically uses the **normal** font for values of **100, 200, 300, 400, 500** and the **bold** font for values of **600, 700, 800, 900**.

CSS also provides the keywords **bolder** and **lighter** for the purpose of moving up or down the font-weight ladder by single steps – but where the browser only recognizes two fonts, one for normal text and the other for bold text, these simply have the same effect as the **normal** and **bold** keywords.

Don't forget

The **font-weight** numeric values do not need to specify a unit type because they are effectively keywords.

1 Create a HTML document with two paragraphs and a heading containing spanned sections of text

```
<p id = "para-1">This normal weight text can become
<span class = "bold">bold</span> or
<span class = "more">bolder</span>
</p>

<p id = "para-2">This bold weight text can get
<span class = "norm">light</span> or
<span class = "less">lighter</span>
</p>

<h2>...here's a heading with
<span class = "less">lighter</span> text</h2>
```

fontweight.html
(fragment)

2 Save the HTML document then create a linked style sheet containing rules specifying a default font weight for each paragraph

```
p#para-1 { font-weight : 400 }
p#para-2 { font-weight : 700 }
```

fontweight.css

3 Next add style rules specifying font weights for the spanned sections of text

```
span.bold { font-weight: bold }
span.more { font-weight: bolder }
span.norm { font-weight: normal }
span.less { font-weight: lighter }
```

4 Save the style sheet alongside the HTML document then open the web page in a browser to see the sections of text appear in the specified font weights

---

Font Weight

This normal weight text can become **bold** or **bolder**

This **bold weight text can get** light or lighter

...here's a heading with lighter text

Varying font styles

Slanting text

A CSS **font-style** property can request the browser to use a slanting variant of the current font by specifying the **italic** or **oblique** keywords – these are subtly different.

When the **italic** keyword is specified the browser seeks an italicized variant of the current font in its font database. This is an actual font set, similar to the current upright font but graphically different to produce slanting versions of each upright character.

When the **oblique** keyword is specified the browser seeks an oblique variant of the current font in its font database. This may be an actual font set, a slanting version of the current upright font, or alternatively it may be a generated version in which the browser has computed a slanting version of the upright font. Either may be mapped to the **oblique** keyword in the browser font database and called upon by the CSS **font-style** property.

In reality using either **italic** or **oblique** keywords typically produces the same italicized text appearance, and in each case upright text can be resumed by specifying the **normal** keyword to the element's **font-style** property.

Small capitals

A CSS property called **font-variant** can specify a **small-caps** value to allow text characters to be displayed in a popular format using uppercase characters of two different sizes.

Uppercase text in the selected element will appear as large capital characters but lowercase text will appear as smaller capitals. The browser may achieve this effect using a smaller capital from the font set, or by generating a computed smaller version.

Once again regular text can be resumed by specifying the **normal** keyword to the **font-variant** property.

Hot tip

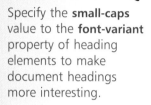

Specify the **small-caps** value to the **font-variant** property of heading elements to make document headings more interesting.

1. Create a HTML document with two paragraphs and a heading containing spanned sections of text

```
<p id = "para-1">This normal style text can become
<span class = "ital">italicized</span> or
<span class = "oblq">oblique</span> </p>

<p id = "para-2">This italic style text can become
<span class = "reg">normal</span> </p>

<h2>...And Here's a
<span class="reg-caps">Heading</span>
with Small Caps</h2>
```

fontstyle.html
(fragment)

2. Save the HTML document then create a linked style sheet containing rules specifying default font styles for each paragraph

```
p#para-1 { font-style : normal }
p#para-2 { font-style : italic }
```

fontstyle.css

3. Next add style rules specifying font styles for the spanned sections of text in the paragraphs

```
span.ital { font-style: italic }
span.oblq  { font-style: oblique }
span.reg { font-style: normal }
```

4. Now add style rules specifying font variants for the heading and its spanned text

```
h2 { font-variant: small-caps }
span.reg-caps { font-variant : normal }
```

5. Save the style sheet alongside the HTML document then open the web page in a browser to see the sections of text appear in the specified font styles and variants

Font Style & Variant

This normal style text can become *italicized* or *oblique*

This italic style text can become normal

...AND HERE'S A Heading WITH SMALL CAPS

81

Using the font shorthand

Usefully CSS provides a **font** property to which various font preferences can be specified in a combined single rule stating:

font-style | font-variant | font-weight | font-size | font-family

Appropriate values can be assigned to each part of the combined **font** shorthand property. For example, like this:

p { font : italic small-caps bold medium "Times", serif }

The first three values for the **font-style**, **font-variant**, and **font-weight** properties may appear in any order. Optionally values for each one of these properties may be completely omitted and a **normal** value will be automatically assumed.

It is important to recognize that values not explicitly specified will still have a **normal** value applied – no value is inherited from the containing element, and this can produce some unexpected results. For example, a style rule selecting a span element within a containing paragraph element styled by the rule above might look like this:

span { font : large cursive }

The values explicitly specified in this rule will be applied to the **font-size** and **font-family** properties of the span element, and a **normal** value will be applied to its **font-style**, **font-variant**, and **font-weight** properties – so text within the span element does not inherit the **italic**, **small-caps**, or **bold** values from the paragraph.

One further possibility available with a combined **font** rule is the option to specify a **line-height** (the spacing between each line) by adding a forward slash and unit value after the **font-weight** value. This is useful to establish a common standard line spacing where various font sizes appear.

1. Create a HTML document containing a paragraph with several spanned sections of text
```
<p class = "general">
<span class = "header">The Sneakers Game</span><br>
In 1934 the
<span class = "giant">New York Giants</span> beat the
<span class="bears">Chicago Bears</span>, by
<span class = "score">30-13</span>,
in nine-degree temperatures
[ <span class="stadium">at the Polo Grounds</span> ]
in a game that has become famous as the "Sneakers
Game." With the <span class ="giant">Giants</span>
trailing <span class = "score">10-3</span> at the half,
head coach <span class = "coach">Steve Owen</span>
provided his squad with basketball shoes to increase
traction on the icy turf. The team responded with four
touchdowns in the second half to turn the game into a
<span class = "giant">Giants</span> rout. </p>
```

font.html
(fragment)

2. Save the HTML document then create a linked style sheet with rules for the paragraph and span elements
```
p.general { font : normal small/1.3em "Courier",monospace }
span.header { font : 350% "Pristina", cursive }
span.giant { font : small-caps large "Castellar", fantasy }
span.bears { font : large "Arial", sans-serif }
span.score { font : bold small "Verdana", sans-serif }
span.stadium { font : italic medium "Arial", sans-serif }
span.coach { font : medium "Comic Sans MS", cursive }
```

font.css

3. Save the style sheet alongside the HTML document then open the web page in a browser to see the font styles

Font

The Sneakers Game

In 1934 the NEW YORK GIANTS beat the Chicago Bears, by 30-13, in nine-degree temperatures [*at the Polo Grounds*] in a game that has become famous as the "Sneakers Game." With the GIANTS trailing 10-3 at the half, head coach Steve Owen provided his squad with basketball shoes to increase traction on the icy turf. The team responded with four touchdowns in the second half to turn the game into a GIANTS rout.

Hot tip

Always use the **font** shorthand property rather than the individual **font-style**, **font-variant**, **font-weight**, **font-size**, and **font-family** properties.

Aligning text

English language text in a paragraph is normally horizontally aligned to the left edge of the paragraph and this is the default behavior to display text in a paragraph element's content box.

Additionally CSS provides a **text-align** property that can explicitly specify how text should be horizontally aligned within the paragraph element's content box using the keywords **left, center, right,** or **justify**. As expected the **left** value aligns each line to the paragraph's left edge, the **right** value aligns each line to the paragraph's right edge, and the **center** value aligns each line centrally between both edges.

Perhaps more interestingly the **justify** value aligns each full line to both left and right edges of the content box and adjusts the spacing between characters and words to make each line the same length.

In displaying lines of text the browser automatically computes the line height to suit the content size – typically this will be the height of the font x 1.2. The browser then displays the text vertically centered in invisible "line boxes" of the computed height.

The CSS **vertical-align** property can explicitly specify how text should be vertically aligned using the keywords **baseline, sub,** and **super**. The **baseline** value specifies central vertical alignment, the default behavior. The **sub** and **super** values increase the boundaries of the outer container in which the line box exists and shift the text down or up respectively to display subscript or superscript.

Content can also be shifted up or down by specifying positive or negative unit values, or percentage values, to the **vertical-align** property. Alternatively the **top, middle,** and **bottom** keywords can specify vertical alignment with top-most, middle, or bottom-most content.

Two other keywords of **text-top** and **text-bottom** can be specified to the **vertical-align** property in order to vertically align other inline content boxes, such as those of image elements, to the top or bottom edge of a line box.

84

1 Create a HTML document containing three paragraphs
```
<p>Enjoy the sunsets, the restaurants, the fishing, the
diving... the lifestyle of the Florida Keys!</p>

<p id="equalize">Enjoy the sunsets, the restaurants, the
fishing, the diving... the lifestyle of the Florida Keys!</p>

<p>Line
<span class="up">Superscript</span>
<span class="down">Subscript</span>
<span class="top">Top</span></p>
```

align.html
(fragment)

2 Save the HTML document then create a linked style
sheet containing a rule to specify the font and colors
```
p, span { font : medium monospace ;
            background : yellow ; border : 1px solid red }
```

align.css

3 Next add a rule to horizontally justify the text within the
second paragraph's content box
```
p#equalize { text-align : justify }
```

4 Now add rules to adjust the vertical alignment of spanned
text within the third paragraph
```
span.up { vertical-align : super }
span.down { vertical-align : sub }
span.top { vertical-align : top }
```

5 Save the style sheet alongside the HTML document then
open the web page in a browser to see the alignments

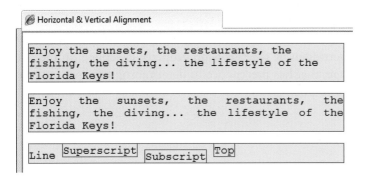

Indenting & spacing text

One of the most common features of printed text is the indentation of the first line of each paragraph to improve readability. This can be easily accomplished for text in HTML paragraphs using the **text-indent** property to specify an indentation size, such as **5em**.

Alternatively the indentation value may be specified as a percentage where the browser will indent an amount relative to the total line length. For example, given a paragraph element within a "div" container element of **500px** width, specifying a **text-indent** value of **10%** would indent the start of the first line by **50px** (500 x 10% = 50).

It is also possible to specify negative values for the **text-indent** property but this can produce inconsistent results so is best avoided.

The amount of space between each word can be adjusted from the **normal** default spacing by explicitly specifying a value to the CSS **word-spacing** property. Note that the specified value is added to the default spacing to increase the space. For example, specifying a unit value of **5em** increases the space to **normal+5em**, not a spacing of **5em** overall.

Similarly the amount of space between each letter can be adjusted from the **normal** default spacing by explicitly specifying a value to the CSS **letter-spacing** property. This also adds the specified value onto the default spacing to determine the total space. For example, specifying a unit value of **5em** increases the space to **normal+5em**, not a spacing of **5em** overall.

Both **word-spacing** and **letter-spacing** properties accept the **normal** keyword to resume normal spacing. Also they may both be overridden by the **text-align** property, described on the previous page, that has precedence in determining the appearance of the entire line.

1 Create a HTML document with two paragraphs containing spanned text

```
<p>The Geologic Story at the
<span class="spread">Grand Canyon</span>
attracts the attention of the world for many reasons, but
perhaps its greatest significance lies in the geologic record
preserved and exposed here.</p>

<p>The rocks at
<span class="spread">Grand Canyon</span>
are not inherently unique but the
<span class="space">variety of rocks clearly exposed
present a complex geologic story.</span> </p>
```

space.html
(fragment)

2 Save the HTML document then create a linked style sheet containing a rule to indent the start of each paragraph

```
p { text-indent : 5em }
```

space.css

3 Next add a style rule to increase the letter spacing and set a background color on two spanned sections of text

```
span.spread { letter-spacing : 1em ; background : yellow }
```

4 Now add a style rule to increase the word spacing and set a background color on the other spanned text

```
span.space { word-spacing : 1.5em ; background : aqua }
```

5 Save the style sheet alongside the HTML document then open the web page in a browser to see the indentations and spacing

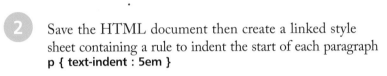

Decorating text

Style rules can add decorative lines to text content using the CSS **text-decoration** property with keywords **underline**, **overline**, and **line-through**. These behave as expected adding a line below, a line above, and a line through the text respectively.

The **blink** keyword may also be specified to the **text-decoration** property to cause the browser to repeatedly hide then display the text, blinking it on and off.

More usefully, the CSS **none** keyword can be specified to the **text-decoration** property to prevent unwanted decorations appearing – this is particularly popular for displaying hyperlinks without their usual default underline.

Multiple keywords can be specified to the **text-decoration** property as a space-separated list to apply multiple decorations to the text.

An additional way to enhance text with CSS is available using the **text-transform** property to specify capitalization in the selected element with the keywords **uppercase**, **lowercase**, or **capitalize**.

Don't forget

Some users may not recognize hyperlinks if their default underline is removed.

decor.html
(fragment)

1. Create a HTML document with a paragraph containing spanned text and another paragraph containing hyperlinks, separated by a ruled line

```
<p id="para-1">You know that it's
<span class = "under caps">important</span>
when<br>it is
<span class = "under">underlined</span>
<br>and that it's been
<span class = "thru caps">cancelled</span>
when<br>it has been
<span class = "thru">struck through</span>
<br>but you also must remember to<br><br>
<span class = "rails upper">read between the lines</span>
<br><br>for not all of man's intentions
<br>are plain communications.<br>
<span id = "sig" class = "lower">MIKE MCGRATH</span>
</p>

<hr>

<p>
<a href = "http://w3c.org">Regular link</a> |
<a class = "plain" href = "http://w3c.org">Plain link</a>
</p>
```

2 Save the HTML document then create a linked style sheet with rules to specify fonts and colors

decor.css

```
#para-1 { font : medium "Courier", monospace ;
                          background : #CCCCFF }

#sig { font : xx-large "Lucida Handwriting", cursive ;
                          color : purple }
```

3 Next add style rules to decorate spanned text with lines

```
span.under { text-decoration : underline }
span.thru { text-decoration : line-through }
span.rails { text-decoration : overline underline blink }
```

4 Now add style rules to transform the case of spanned text

```
span.lower { text-transform : lowercase }
span.upper { text-transform : uppercase }
span.caps { text-transform : capitalize }
```

5 Finally add a style rule to remove the default underline from a hyperlink

```
a.plain { text-decoration : none }
```

6 Save the style sheet alongside the HTML document then open the web page in a browser to see the text decorations and case transformations

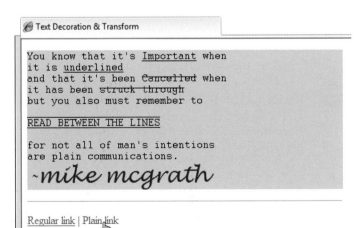

Beware

Avoid using the **blink** value as blinking text is despised by many users, and is not supported by default in some browsers.

Governing space & direction

The default treatment of whitespace within text content is to collapse multiple spaces into a single space, but this can be controlled with the CSS **white-space** property. Specifying the **pre** keyword preserves all spaces as they appear in the original text, including any line breaks. Conversely, the automatic wrapping of text in a block can be prevented by specifying the **no-wrap** keyword. Additionally the **pre-wrap** keyword can be specified to preserve spaces while still allowing text to wrap normally, or the **pre-line** keyword can be specified to collapse multiple spaces while preserving line breaks.

The default left-to-right direction of text lines can be changed to right-to-left by specifying the **rtl** keyword to the CSS **direction** property and the normal direction resumed with the **ltr** keyword.

Interestingly, when the line direction is changed with the **rtl** keyword the words appear from right-to-left but the order of English language characters are preserved so that each word still reads correctly left-to-right.

This intelligent feature also allows text to be presented in different directions on a single line. For example, to incorporate words in languages that are read right-to-left such as Hebrew and Arabic. The browser examines the Unicode value of each character using a complex BiDirectional algorithm to determine which direction each word should be displayed – those characters from right-to-left languages are automatically displayed in that direction, even if written logically from left-to-right in the HTML source code. The automatic BiDirectional algorithm can be turned off however by specifying the **bidi-override** keyword to a **unicode-bidi** property.

Hot tip

You can discover more about Unicode online at **www.unicode.org** and more on character entities at **www.w3.org**.

90

direction.html
(fragment)

1. Create a HTML document with a paragraph containing Hebrew character entities and stepped whitespace
```
<p>Hebrew "Congratulations" with mazel tov:
&#1502;&#1494;&#1500;  [mazel]
  + &#1496;&#1493;&#1489;  [tov]
    = &#1502;&#1494;&#1500;  &#1496;&#1493;&#1489;;
</p>
```

2. Next begin a definition list with the same entities
```
<dl>
<dt>LTR Default Direction (lines begin at the LEFT):</dt>
<dd class = "ltr">&#1502;&#1494;&#1500; [mazel]
&#1496;&#1493;&#1489; [tov]</dd>
```

3 Now add two more definitions to complete the list, again
featuring the same Hebrew character entities

```
<dt>RTL Custom Direction (lines begin at the RIGHT):</dt>
<dd class = "rtl">&#1502;&#1494;&#1500; [mazel]
&#1496;&#1493;&#1489; [tov]</dd>

<dt>LTR Explicit Direction + BiDirectional Override:</dt>
<dd class = "bidi-off ltr">No longer reads as mazel tov :
&#1502;&#1494;&#1500; &#1496;&#1493;&#1489;</dd>
</dl>
```

4 Save the HTML document then create a linked style
sheet with a style rule to color element backgrounds

```
p,dd { background : yellow }
```

direction.css

5 Next add a style rule to preserve whitespace in paragraphs

```
p { whitespace : pre }
```

6 Now add style rules to set the text directions of each
definition in the list

```
dd.ltr { direction : ltr }
dd.rtl { direction : rtl }
dd.bidi-off { unicode-bidi : bidi-override }
```

7 Save the style sheet alongside the HTML document
then open the web page in a browser to see the preserved
whitespace and various text directions

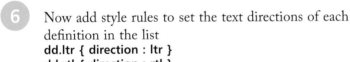

Beware

Generally the default
treatment of right-to-
left language characters
achieves the desired
effect. In practice
overriding the Unicode
BiDirectional algorithm is
seldom needed.

Summary

- The **font-family** property can suggest specific fonts by name and also specify a generic font family as either **serif, sans-serif, monospace, cursive,** or **fantasy**

- Font size can be specified using keywords such as **large,** absolute sizes such as **12pt,** or relative sizes such as **larger**

- Thickness of text can be specified to the **font-weight** property using keywords such as **bold,** or numeric values such as **700**

- Slanting text can be created by specifying the **italic** or **oblique** keywords to the **font-style** property

- Specifying a **small-caps** value to the **font-variant** property causes lowercase characters to appear as small capital letters

- The **font** shorthand property can be used to specify values for the **font-style, font-variant, font-weight, font-size,** and **font-family** properties rather than individual rules

- The **font-weight** property may also specify a **line-height** by adding a forward slash and unit size after the weight value

- Horizontal position of text within a content box can be specified to the **text-align** property by keywords such as **center**

- Vertical inline position of text can be specified to the **vertical-align** property using keywords such as **super**

- The **text-indent** property allows the start of each paragraph to be indented by a specified distance

- Text spacing can be adjusted by the **word-spacing** and **letter-spacing** properties

- Lines can be added to text by the **text-decoration** property and the case can be specified to the **text-transform** property

- Specifying **pre** to the **white-space** property preserves spacing

- The **direction** property can control text direction but can be overridden by the **unicode-bidi** property

6 Arranging data

This chapter demonstrates how to arrange data in tables and lists.

Setting table columns

Although web page authors are now discouraged from using HTML tables for page layout (in favor of CSS) tables remain an invaluable format for the presentation of information within the content of a page.

When displaying a HTML table the browser will, by default, automatically create a table layout sized to accommodate its content. This invariably produces a table with columns of varying width where each column width is determined by the widest content of any cell in that column. This process requires the browser to examine the table content in some detail before it can compute the optimum table layout and, especially for large tables, can take some time before the browser is able to draw the table.

CSS provides an alternative that allows the browser to quickly compute a suitable table layout without examining the content of the entire table – a fixed-layout can be specified to the **table-layout** property of a table element with the **fixed** keyword.

In a **fixed** layout the browser need only consider the **width** value of the table itself and the **width** value of the columns and cells on its first row to determine the table layout like this:

- The overall table width will be its specified **width** value or the sum of its column **width** values – whichever is the greater

- A specified column **width** value sets the width for that column

- When there is no specified column **width** value a specified cell **width** value sets the width for that column

- Any columns that have no specified **width** values, for either column or cell, will be sized equally within the table width

Alternatively a style rule can explictly specify that the default table layout scheme should be used, in which the browser computes the column widths according to their content, by assigning an **auto** value to the **table-layout** property.

Where tables include a caption element the position of the caption can be suggested by specifying keywords of **top** or **bottom** to the table element's CSS **caption-side** property.

1 Create a HTML document containing two tables with similar content

```
<table><caption>Auto Layout</caption>
<tr><td>Text content</td>
<td>Text content wider than 130px</td>
<td>Text content</td></tr></table>

<table class = "fix"><caption>Fixed Layout</caption>
<tr><td>Text content</td>
<td>Text content wider than 130px</td>
<td>Text content</td></tr></table>
```

table.html
(fragment)

2 Save the HTML document then create a style sheet containing a rule to specify table width and its features

```
table { width : 390px ; border : 3px dashed blue ;
caption-side : top ; text-align : center ; margin : 0 0 20px }
```

table.css

3 Next add style rules to color each table cell and caption

```
td { border : 3px solid red ; background : yellow }
caption { background : aqua }
```

4 Now add a style rule to specify a fixed size column scheme for the second table

```
table.fix { table-layout : fixed }
```

5 Save the style sheet alongside the HTML document then open the web page in a browser to see tables drawn with both automatic and fixed layout schemes

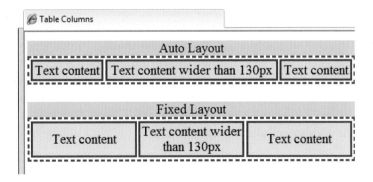

Spacing table cells

The distance between table cell borders can be specified as a unit value to the CSS **border-spacing** property. This easily allows cells to be spread some distance apart throughout a table.

A single specified **border-spacing** value will be applied uniformly to all cell separations – in much the same way as with the HTML cellspacing attribute.

CSS provides greater flexibility however, by allowing two values to be specified to the **border-spacing** property as a space-separated list. The first will be applied to the horizontal spacing, at the left and right of each table cell, and the second will be applied to the vertical spacing at the top and bottom of each cell. This means that different distances can be specified for the horizontal and vertical spacing throughout a table.

Another possibility offered by CSS is the ability to hide table cells that contain no content. These frequently occur due to the grid format of tables, which does not always conveniently match the number of cells required. For example, displaying nine content items in a table of five rows and two columns.

Creating a style rule with the CSS **empty-cells** property specifying a **hide** value will cause the browser to not display the border and background of any cell that contains absolutely no content. Cells that contain any content at all, even if it's simply a ** ** (non-breaking space entity) will still be visible.

Conversely a style rule can explicitly ensure that empty cells are displayed by specifying a **show** value to the **empty-cells** property.

Empty cells that are hidden do continue to have a presence in the table layout inasmuch as their **border-spacing** values are preserved. For example, where the **border-spacing** property is set to **20px**, and the **empty-cells** property specifies a **hide** value, a single empty cell is not displayed but the surrounding cells remain 40 pixels apart – rather than just a distance of 20 pixels that would exist if the hidden cell did not exist.

Beware

Older versions of Internet Explorer, prior to IE8, do not support the **border-spacing** property.

1 Create a HTML document containing two tables with similar content
```
<table>
<tr><td>1</td><td></td><td>3</td></tr>
</table>

<table class = "space">
<tr><td>1</td><td></td><td>3</td></tr>
</table>
```

hide.html
(fragment)

2 Save the HTML document then create a style sheet containing a rule to specify table width and its features
```
table { width : 350px ;
               margin : 20px ; border : 3px dotted red }
```

hide.css

3 Next add a style rule to color each table cell and border
```
td { border : 3px solid blue ; background : aqua }
```

4 Now add a style rule to specify the border spacing and hide empty cells in the second table
```
table.space { border-spacing : 20px ; empty-cells : hide }
```

5 Save the style sheet alongside the HTML document then open the web page in a browser to see tables drawn with both visible and hidden empty cells

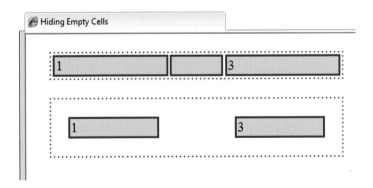

Collapsing table borders

The borders of adjacent table borders, and table cell borders, can be made to "collapse" into a single border by specifying the **collapse** keyword to the CSS **border-collapse** property. This requires the browser to perform a series of evaluations, comparing the existing borders, to determine how the collapsed border should appear:

- **Visibility Evaluation:** where one of the borders to be collapsed has a **border-style** value of **hidden** that value takes precedence – so the collapsed border at that location will be hidden

- **Width Evaluation:** where two visible borders with different **border-width** values are to be collapsed the highest value takes precedence – so the collapsed border will be the greater width

- **Style Evaluation:** where two visible borders of equal width are to be collapsed their **border-style** value sets the precedence in the descending status order of **double, solid, dashed, dotted, ridge, outset, groove, inset** – so the collapsed border at that location will be in the style of highest status. For example, a **double** style wins out over a **solid** style

- **Color Evaluation:** where two visible borders of equal width and identical style are to be collapsed the **border-color** value is determined in the descending status order of cell, row, row group, column, column group, table – so the collapsed border will be in the color of highest status. For example, the cell **border-color** wins out over the table **border-color** value

The effect of collapsing borders where a table **border-width** of **2px** is compared to a cell **border-width** of **5px** means that the collapsed **border-width** will be 5 pixels – the greater width.

In comparing adjacent **border-style** values of **dotted** and **double** the collapsed **border-style** will be double – the higher status.

Similarly, comparing adjacent **border-style** values of **dotted** and **solid** the collapsed **border-style** will be solid – the higher status.

Don't forget

The **separate** keyword can also be specified to the **border-collapse** property – to explicitly prevent collapsing borders.

1 Create a HTML document containing two tables with similar content

```
<table><tr>
<td class = "twin">1</td>
<td class = "dots">2</td>
<td class = "full">3</td>
</tr></table>

<table class = "fold"><tr>
<td class = "twin">1</td>
<td class = "dots">2</td>
<td class = "full">3</td>
</tr></table>
```

collapse.html
(fragment)

2 Save the HTML document then create a style sheet containing a rule to specify table width and its features

```
table { width : 350px ; height : 60px ; margin : 20px }
```

collapse.css

3 Next add style rules to specify the size and color of the table border and each table cell

```
table { border : 2px solid black }
td.twin { border : 5px double green }
td.dots { border : 5px dotted red }
td.full { border : 5px solid blue }
```

4 Now add a style rule to collapse the borders of the second table

```
table.fold { border-collapse : collapse }
```

5 Save the style sheet alongside the HTML document then open the web page in a browser to see tables drawn with both regular and collapsed borders

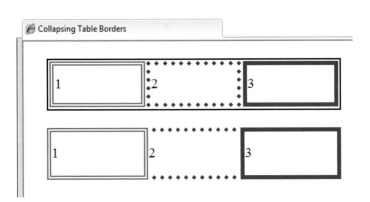

Assigning table features

The CSS **display** property can accept a range of values to specify that a selected element should be treated as a table component – emulating the default behavior of HTML tags that a browser automatically applies to table components:

HTML Tag	CSS Equivalent
<table>	**table**
<tr>	**table-row**
<thead>	**table-header-group**
<tbody>	**table-row-group**
<tfoot>	**table-footer-group**
<col>	**table-column**
<colgroup>	**table-column-group**
<th>	**} table-cell**
<td>	
<caption>	**table-caption**

The CSS values that can be specified to the **display** property are listed in the table above together with the HTML tag they most closely represent. These can be used to specify table features to elements of an XML document so a browser will display their content as if it was a HTML table.

xtable.xml

1 Create an XML document that nominates a CSS style sheet to format its element content

```
<?xml version="1.0" encoding="UTF-8"?>
<?xml-stylesheet href="xtable.css" type="text/css"?>
<liga><cap>La Liga Top 3</cap>
 <hdrs>
  <lbl>Position</lbl> <lbl>Team</lbl> <lbl>Points</lbl>
 </hdrs>
 <rows>
  <team> <pos>1</pos> <name>Barcelona</name>
  <pts>84</pts> </team>
  <team> <pos>2</pos> <name>Real Madrid</name>
  <pts>80</pts> </team>
  <team> <pos>3</pos> <name>Villareal</name>
  <pts>65</pts> </team>
 </rows>
</liga>
```

2 Save the XML document then create a style sheet with rules that assign table characteristics to the XML tags

```
cap { display : table-caption }
liga { display : table }
hdrs { display: table-header-group }
rows { display: table-row-group }
team { display: table-row }
name, pos,pts, lbl { display: table-cell }
```

xtable.css

3 Next add a style rule that specifies the table features

```
liga { margin : auto ; margin-top : 20px ; width : 300px ;
            border-spacing : 3px ; border : 8px ridge lime }
```

4 Now add style rules to color the headers and row cells

```
hdrs { background : lime }
rows { background: aqua }
```

5 Save the style sheet alongside the XML document then open the document in a browser to see the table

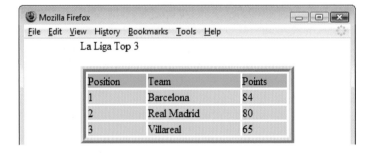

Beware

This example is illustrated in Firefox and Opera browsers as Internet Explorer does not fully support these features at the time of writing.

Choosing list markers

A list "marker" indicates the beginning of an item in a list – typically a bullet in an unordered <ul> list, or an incrementing number in an <ol> ordered list. The browser conducts an item count in each case but usually only uses this to number the items in an ordered list display.

The CSS **list-style-type** property can specify an alternative type of marker for any list – so unordered lists can have numbered markers and ordered lists can have bullet-points if so desired.

Keywords allow the bullet marker type to be specified as **disc**, **circle**, or **square**, and number marker types as **lower-roman**, **upper-roman**, **decimal**, or **decimal-leading-zero**.

Alphabetical marker types can be specified with the **lower-latin**, **upper-latin**, and **lower-greek** keywords. Additionally the CSS specification provides keywords for other alphabets such as **armenian** and **georgian** – but a suitable font is needed for the marker to be displayed correctly by the web browser.

The **list-style-type** property can also specify a **none** value to explicitly suppress the markers so they will not be displayed, although they do remain in the item count.

Optionally an image may be specified as a marker by stating its path in the parentheses of a **url()** value to the **list-style-image** property.

markers.html
(fragment)

1 Create a HTML document containing three headings and several ordered lists

```
<h3>Alphabetical list marker types:</h3>
<ol id = "list-0"><li>lower-latin<li>...<li>...<li>...</ol>
<ol id = "list-1"><li>upper-latin<li>...<li>...<li>...</ol>
<ol id = "list-2"><li>lower-greek<li>...<li>...<li>...</ol>
<h3>Bullet list marker types:</h3>
<ol id = "list-3"><li>disc<li>...<li>...<li>...</ol>
<ol id = "list-4"><li>circle<li>...<li>...<li>...</ol>
<ol id = "list-5"><li>square<li>...<li>...<li>...</ol>
<ol id = "list-6"><li>image<li>...<li>...<li>...</ol>
<h3>Numerical list marker types:</h3>
<ol id = "list-7"><li>lower-roman<li>...<li>...<li>...</ol>
<ol id = "list-8"><li>upper-roman<li>...<li>...<li>...</ol>
<ol id = "list-9"><li>decimal<li>...<li>...<li>...</ol>
<ol id = "list-10"><li>decimal-leading-zero
                         <li>...<li>...<li>...</ol>
```

...cont'd

2 Save the HTML document then create a linked style sheet with rules to specify heading and list features
```
h3 { clear : left ; margin : 0 }
ol {      margin : 0 ; border : 1px solid black ; float : left ;
          background : aqua ; padding : 0 0 0 10px }
li { margin : 0 0 20px ; background : yellow }
```

markers.css

3 Next add style rules to specify alphabetical list markers
```
ol#list-0 { list-style-type: lower-latin }
ol#list-1 { list-style-type: upper-latin }
ol#list-2 { list-style-type: lower-greek }
```

4 Now add style rules to specify bullet list markers
```
ol#list-3 { list-style-type: disc}
ol#list-4 { list-style-type: circle }
ol#list-5 { list-style-type: square }
ol#list-6 { list-style-image : url(tick.png) }
```

5 Finally add style rules to specify numerical list markers
```
ol#list-7 { list-style-type: lower-roman }
ol#list-8 { list-style-type: upper-roman }
ol#list-9 { list-style-type: decimal }
ol#list-10 { list-style-type: decimal-leading-zero }
```

6 Save the style sheet alongside the HTML document then open the web page in a browser to see the list markers

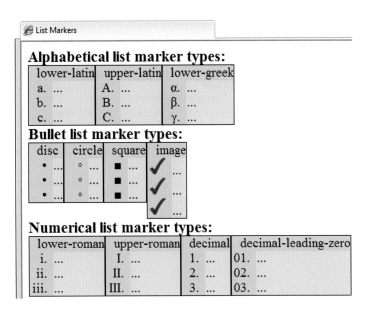

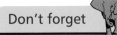

Don't forget

Both numerical and alphabetical markers display the incrementing item count.

103

Positioning list markers

Typically to display a list the browser creates a block-level content box for the entire list and inline content boxes for each list item. Typically a left margin insets the list item content boxes and each marker appears up against the right edge of this margin area – outside the list item content boxes.

The position of the marker may be explicitly specified to the **list-style-position** property using **inside** or **outside** keywords to determine whether the markers should appear inside the list item content boxes.

Rather than creating separate style rules for the **list-style-type**, **list-style-image**, and **list-style-position** properties it is simpler to use the CSS shorthand technique that may specify a value for each property as a space-separated list to the **list-style** property. The values may appear in any order and where any value is omitted the default value for that property will be assumed.

Lists of either type may be nested with their marker position and type specified independently:

list.html
(fragment)

1 Create a HTML document containing three lists plus one nested list

```
<ol class = "outside-markers">
 <li>List<li>Markers<li>Outside content box
</ol>

<ol class = "inside-markers">
 <li>List<li>Markers<li>Inside content box
</ol>

<ul>
 <li>List<li>Style
 <ol class = "inside-markers">
 <li>List<li>Markers<li>Inside content box
 </ol><li>Shorthand
</ul>
```

list.css

2 Save the HTML document then create a linked style sheet containing rules to show the list boundaries

```
li { background : yellow }
ol,ul { border : 2px solid red }
```

3 Next add a style rule to specify that some ordered list markers should appear outside the list item content boxes
ol.outside-markers { list-style-position : outside }

4 Now add a style rule to specify that other ordered list markers should appear inside the list item content boxes
ol.inside-markers { list-style-position : inside }

5 Finally add a shorthand style rule that specifies the position, image, and bullet type for the unordered list
ul { list-style : url(lilguy.gif) outside square }

6 Save the style sheet alongside the HTML document then open the web page in a browser to see the lists

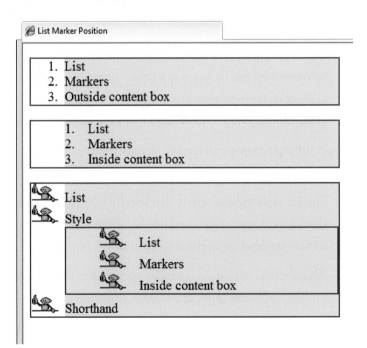

Hot tip

Nested lists can specify they should adopt the **list-style** of the containing element using the **inherit** keyword or suppress markers with the **none** keyword.

Don't forget

The **square** marker type specified by the shorthand rule will be used when the specified image is not available.

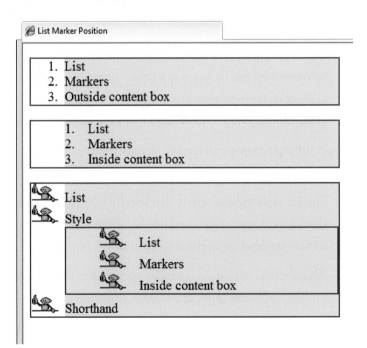

Summary

- When the **table-layout** property specifies a **fixed** layout the browser need only assess the **width** value of the table and the **width** of the cells on its first row so can quickly draw the table

- The **caption-side** property can specify whether the table caption should appear at the **top** or **bottom** of the table

- A **border-spacing** property can specify the distance between table cell borders

- Cells containing absolutely no content can be hidden by specifying a **hide** value to the **empty-cells** property

- Adjacent borders of a table and its cells can be combined into a single border by specifying the **collapse** keyword to the **border-collapse** property

- The **display** property can specify that a selected element should be treated by the browser as a table component using **table**, **table-row**, **table-header-group**, **table-row-group**, **table-cell**, **table-footer-group**, **table-column**, or **table-caption** keywords

- A **list-style-type** property can specify the type of bullet marker to be used for list items with **disc**, **circle**, or **square** keywords

- The **list-style-type** property can specify that each list item should have numerical markers using the **lower-roman, upper-roman, decimal,** or **decimal-leading-zero** keywords

- Alphabetical list markers can be specified to the **list-style-type** property as **lower-latin, upper-latin,** or **lower-greek**

- An image can be used as a list marker by stating its path in the **url()** value specified to the **list-style-image** property

- Specifying a value of **inside** or **outside** to the **list-style-position** determines whether markers appear inside the content box

- The **list-style** property can specify the individual **list-style-type**, **list-style-image**, and **list-style-position** properties as CSS shorthand

7 Generating effects

This chapter demonstrates how to generate content and create dynamic effects.

Inserting text enhancements

CSS provides four "pseudo-elements" of **:before**, **:after**, **:first-letter**, and **:first-line** that can be included in the style rule selector to enhance the actual content of a selected element.

The **:before** and **:after** pseudo-elements place generated content around the original content and appear in the selector immediately after the element name. For example, a selector of **p:before** generates content before the content of each paragraph.

The **:before** and **:after** pseudo-elements specify the content to be generated to a **content** property in the style rule declaration. Most simply the declaration specifies a string of text to be generated. The string must be enclosed within quote marks though these will not be included in the generated content, but spaces in the string will be preserved in the generated content. Alternatively the **content** property can specify the keywords **open-quote** or **close-quote** to explicitly generate quotes around original content.

Generated content is not limited to text strings as the special **url()** keyword can be used to specify non-textual content to the **content** property by stating the path to a resource within the parentheses. For example, a declaration might specify an image to be generated using **content : url(image.png)** to generate the image as content.

Additionally the special **attr()** keyword can be used to specify to the **content** property the name of an attribute within the selected element whose assigned value should be generated as content. For example, a declaration might specify an attribute whose value should be generated using **content : attr(src)** to generate the value of the selected element's "src" attribute as content.

Multiple items to be generated can be specified to the **content** property as a space-separated list – using any of the above.

Don't forget

In CSS all pseudo-elements begin with a colon character.

pseudo.html
(fragment)

1. Create a HTML document with five paragraphs that each contain a hyperlink to the same resource
```
<p>Get more <a href = "info.pdf">info</a> here</p>
<p>Get more
   <a href = "info.pdf" class = "quo">info</a> here</p>
<p>Get more
   <a href = "info.pdf" class = "lnk">info</a> here</p>
<p>Get more
   <a href = "info.pdf" class = "pdf">info</a> here</p>
<p>Get more
   <a href = "info.pdf" class = "att">info</a> here</p>
```

...cont'd

2   Save the HTML document then create a linked style sheet containing rules to add text characters on colored backgrounds before and after the content of each paragraph
p:before { content : "*" ; background : yellow }**
p:after { content : "!!!" ; background : aqua }

pseudo.css

3   Next add rules to insert colored quotes around a link
a[href].quo:before { content : open-quote ; color : red }
a[href].quo:after { content : close-quote ; color : red }

4   Now add a rule to insert colored text before a link
a[href].lnk:before { content : "[link]: " ; color : orange }

Hot tip

The **:first-letter** and **:first-line** properties target text content within an element – an example using these pseudo-elements appears on page 113.

5   Then add a rule to insert an image after a link
a[href].pdf:after { content : url(pdf-ico.gif) }

6   Finally add a rule to insert a colored attribute value after a link
a[href].att:after { content : " [" attr(href) "] " ;
                                  color : green }

7   Save the style sheet alongside the HTML document then open the web page in a browser to see the content generated by CSS in addition to that in the HTML code

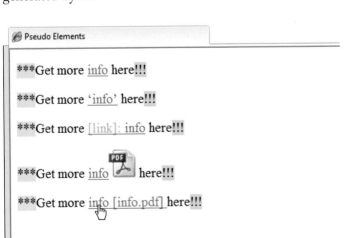

Hot tip

Generated content is added inside the content box of the selected element – so the enhancements to the links in this example become part of the link.

Numbering document sections

The CSS :**before** pseudo-element, introduced in the previous example, can insert generated content to automatically number sections of a HTML document using the special **counter()** keyword. This specifies the name of a counter to be inserted into content within its parentheses.

A counter to count the instances of a selected element must first be created by specifying a chosen name and an incremental value to the **counter-increment** property as a space-separated list.

The counter will begin counting from zero by default and will increment by the specified incremental value for every instance of the selected element. Optionally the explicitly specified incremental value may be omitted from the rule so the value of 1 will be assumed as the incremental value. For example, a declaration of **counter-increment : num** creates a counter named "num" that will start counting from zero and increment by one.

Additionally the counter can be made to resume counting from a number other than the current count number by specifying the counter name and an integer value from which to count as a space-separated list to the **counter-reset** property. Typically this will specify a zero integer value to resume counting afresh.

Once a counter has been created it can be inserted before a selected element as generated content by a CSS pseudo-element.

counter.html
(fragment)

1. Create a HTML document with various headings of two different sizes
```
<h2>Topic</h2>
    <h3>Section</h3>
    <h3>Section</h3>
    <h3>Section</h3>

<h2>Topic</h2>
    <h3 class="restart">Section</h3>
    <h3>Section</h3>
    <h3>Section</h3>
```

counter.css

2. Save the HTML document then create a linked style sheet containing a rule to create a counter for the larger heading elements, which will increment by one
```
h2 { counter-increment : num 1 }
```

3   Next add a style rule to create a counter for the smaller heading elements, which will increment by one
h3 { counter-increment : sub 1 }

4   Now add a style rule to insert the current larger heading counter value before each larger heading and set the counter's background color
h2:before { content : counter(num) " " ;
                                        background : aqua }

5   Then add a style rule to insert both the current larger and smaller heading counter value before each smaller heading and set that background color
h3:before { content : counter(num) "." counter(sub) " " ;
                                        background : lime }

6   Finally add a style rule to reset the smaller heading counter after each larger heading element
h3.restart { counter-reset : sub 0 }

7   Save the style sheet alongside the HTML document then open the web page in a browser to see the generated counter values inserted before each heading

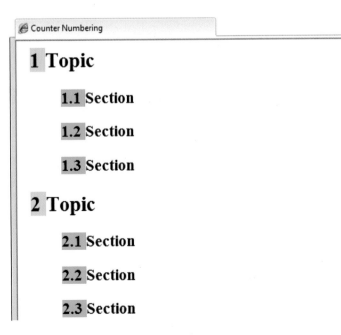

Hot tip

Notice that the generated content in this example includes a space for formatting purposes.

Highlighting important content

In addition to the four pseudo-elements of :**before**, :**after**, :**first-letter**, and :**first-line**, CSS provides a number of pseudo-classes that can be included with the selector in a style rule.

Typically the :**first-child** and :**lang()** pseudo-classes are used to highlight content by changing the text color or background color. It is important to recognize that the :**first-child** pseudo-class acts upon the first selected element contained within an outer element – not the first child element within a selected element.

The :**lang()** pseudo-class can be included in a style rule selector to select an element by its language as an alternative to using the attribute selector technique described on page 28. For example, the selector *:**lang(es)** is equivalent to the selector *[lang="es"] to select all elements that have a **lang** attribute assigned an "es" value denoting Spanish language content. The :**lang()** pseudo-class is more powerful however as it also considers other factors, such as document headers and meta data, to determine the language.

Notice that, unlike the attribute selector, the :**lang()** pseudo-class does not require quote marks around the language specified within its parentheses. Its simpler syntax and greater power make the :**lang()** pseudo-class the preferable method to select elements according to the language of their content.

Unlike pseudo-elements, multiple pseudo-classes can be included in a single selector. For example, **p:first-child:lang(fr)** would select the first paragraph element with French language content that is contained within an outer element.

The :**first-child** and :**lang()** pseudo-classes can often be used in conjunction with the :**first-letter** and :**first-line** pseudo-elements to highlight important content.

highlight.html
(fragment)

1 Create a HTML document with two paragraphs containing spanned sections of text
```
<p>In what was once Texcoco lake, birthplace of
<span>pre-Hispanic civilizations</span>, lies the
<span lang = "es">Ciudad de los Palacios</span>
(City of Palaces) that is today, Mexico City.</p>

<p>Mexico City offers visitors a great many different
interesting sites to visit, from
<span>pre-Columbian Mexico</span> to modern and
<span>cosmopolitan 21st century Mexico</span>.</p>
```

2 Save the HTML document then create a linked style sheet containing a rule to color the first letter of each paragraph
p:first-letter { font-size : 200% ; color : red }

highlight.css

3 Next add a style rule to color the background of the first line in each paragraph
p:first-line { background-color : yellow }

4 Now add a style rule to color the background of elements containing Spanish language content
***:lang(es) { background-color : lime }**

5 Finally add a style rule to color the first section of spanned text within an outer containing element
span:first-child { background-color : aqua }

6 Save the style sheet alongside the HTML document then open the web page in a browser to see the highlighted content

113

Highlighting Content

In what was once Texcoco lake, birthplace of pre-Hispanic civilizations, lies the Ciudad de los Palacios (City of Palaces) that is today, Mexico City.

Mexico City offers visitors a great many different interesting sites to visit, from pre-Columbian Mexico to modern and cosmopolitan 21st century Mexico.

Hot tip

Notice that the **:first-child** class has more weight than the **:first-line** element – so part of the first line is colored by the **:first-child** rule's declaration.

Providing special cursors

The CSS **cursor** property can specify the type of cursor to display when the pointer hovers over a selected element. Its default value of **auto** allows the browser to determine which cursor to display, but specifying a **default** keyword will explicitly force the browser to use the operating system's default cursor.

Alternative cursor keywords, together with the cursor icons they represent in the Windows operating system, are listed below:

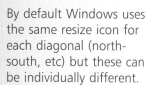
114

Keyword	Cursor	Keyword	Cursor
default	↖	n-resize	↕
pointer	👆	ne-resize	⤢
crosshair	+	e-resize	↔
move	✥	se-resize	⬊
text	I	s-resize	↕
wait	⌛	sw-resize	⤢
progress	↖⌛	w-resize	↔
help	↖?	nw-resize	⬊

Traditionally the **pointer** cursor icon indicates a hyperlink, the **move** cursor icon indicates an item that can be dragged, and the **text** cursor icon indicates a component in which text can be selected. As most users are familiar with these cursor conventions it is best to adhere to them.

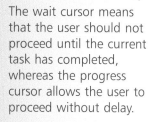
In addition to system cursor icons the **cursor** property can specify an image for use as a custom cursor icon by stating its path within the parentheses of the **url()** keyword. Multiple images may be specified, as a comma-separated list, but the list should always end with a regular cursor keyword to specify which system cursor icon to use if the specified images are unavailable.

1 Create a HTML document containing two paragraphs
```
<p class ="help-cursor">Browser defined help cursor</p>
<p class ="arrow-cursor">
         Custom arrow cursor (or browser default)</p>
```

cursor.html (fragment)

2 Save the HTML document then create a linked style sheet with a rule to specify paragraph height and color
```
p { border : 1px solid black ; height : 50px ;
                           background: yellow }
```

cursor.css

3 Next add style rules to specify cursors for the paragraphs
```
p.help-cursor { cursor : help }
p.arrow-cursor{ cursor : url(blue-arrow.cur), default }
```

blue-arrow.cur

4 Save the style sheet alongside the HTML document then hover the pointer over each paragraph to see the cursors

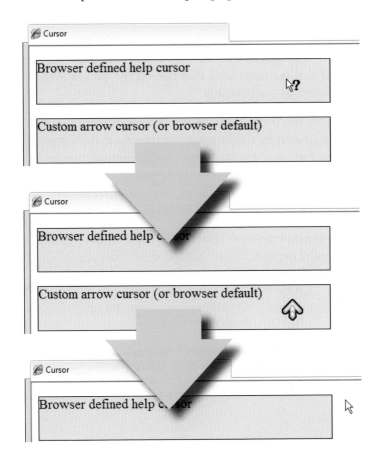

Outlining page components

Components of a HTML document can be emphasized using the CSS **outline** property to draw an outline around selected elements. Unusually, the outline is drawn around the content of the selected elements on a layer above the content box – so it does not influence the box model in any way.

The **outline** shorthand property is similar to the **border** shorthand property inasmuch as it can accept very nearly all the the same values to specify style, width, and color, as a space-separated list.

As with the **border** property a style must always be explicitly specified to the **outline** property but the width and color values may be omitted. There are also **outline-style**, **outline-width**, and **outline-color** properties to specify individual property values.

Unlike borders, outlines always have uniform style on each side – so there are no outline properties to specify individual side values, nor can the **outline-style** property have a **hidden** value.

In addition to specifying color in the usual way the **outline-color** property can specify an **invert** keyword to have the browser select a color that contrasts with that behind the outline – so the outline will always be easily visible.

The CSS specifications leave the precise treatment of outlines to be determined by the browser but they do make suggestions as to how they may appear. Surprisingly, the truly unique suggestion is that an outline can be non-rectangular. This does not provide curved outlines (yet) but allows contiguous outlines to disappear leaving a single non-rectangular outline around the content edges.

The suggested position at which to draw an **outline**, relative to the box model beneath, is just outside the border edge.

outline.html
(fragment)

1. Create a HTML document with one heading and a paragraph containing some spanned text
```
<h2>Gold Rush Fever</h2>

<p>By early 1849, gold fever was an epidemic.
<span>Farmers left their fields; merchants closed their
shops; soldiers left their posts - and made plans for
California.</span> Newspapers fanned the fires.</p>
```

...cont'd

2 Save the HTML document then create a linked style sheet containing a rule to specify margin and padding values for the heading and paragraph elements
h2,p { padding : 5px ; width : 300px }

outline.css

3 Next add style rules to specify borders and backgrounds for the heading and paragraph elements
h2 { border : 3px dashed blue ; background : aqua }
p { border : 3px dashed green ; background : yellow }

4 Now add a style rule to add an outline around the spanned text
h2,span { outline : 2px solid red }

5 Save the style sheet alongside the HTML document then open the web page in a browser to see the text outlined

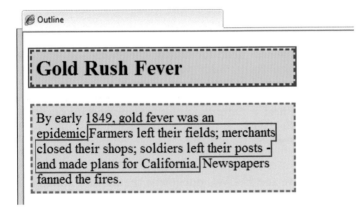

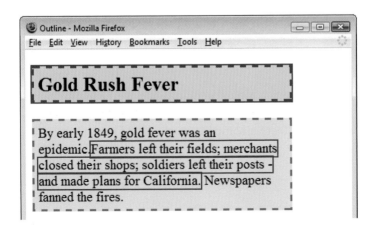

Beware

The CSS specifications do not define how overlapping lines should be treated so their appearance can vary. Notice the difference shown here between this example in Internet Explorer and Firefox.

Indicating current focus

Interactive components of a HTML document comprise those elements that can accept keyboard input, such as a text field, and those that can be activated by a user action, such as a push button or hyperlink. When one of these interactive components is selected by the user, typically by a mouse click or tab key, it is ready to be activated and is said to have "focus".

CSS provides the **:focus** pseudo-class that can be used to apply styling to the element with current focus in a document – in recognition of the user's selection. The styling is removed from that element when the focus shifts to another element, as the user selects a different interactive component.

Indicating the element with current focus is especially useful in lengthy forms with many input fields as it acts as a marker that easily identifies the progress through the form.

focus.html
(fragment)

1. Create a HTML document containing a form with several interactive components

```
<form action="">
<fieldset>
<legend> Send for details </legend>
<label for = "addr">Enter your email address: </label>
<input id = "addr" type = "text">
<input type = "submit" value = "Send">
<a href = "http://samples">Samples Page</a>
</fieldset>
</form>
```

focus.css

2. Save the HTML document then create a linked style sheet with a rule to color input elements when in focus
input:focus { background : lime }

3. Next add a style rule to color hyperlinks when in focus
a:focus { background : aqua }

4. Save the style sheet alongside the HTML document then open the web page in a browser and select each interactive component in turn to see the styles applied

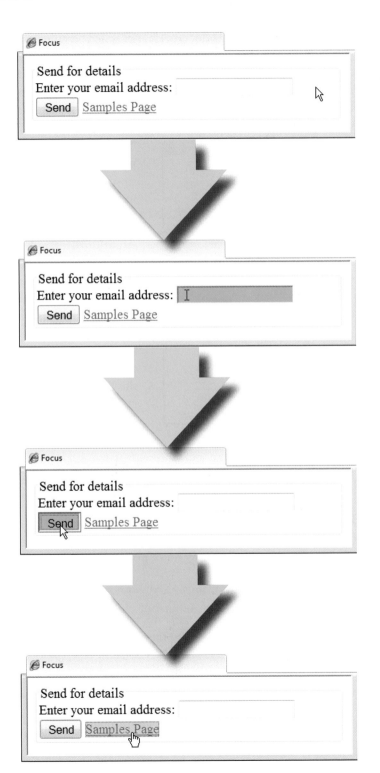

Don't forget

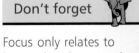

Focus only relates to interactive elements that can receive keyboard input or be somehow activated by the user.

Displaying hyperlink status

Hyperlinks in a HTML document appear in the color designated by the browser's default scheme to indicate their status as either "visited" or "unvisited". The status is determined by comparing the user's browser history and typically uses the colors from Internet Explorer's default scheme, shown below:

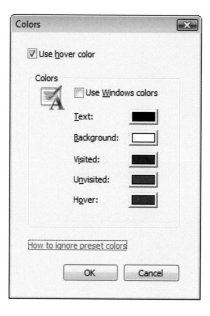

The CSS :link and :visited pseudo-classes can be used to specify different colors to indicate the history status of hyperlinks in a document.

Additionally, the :hover and :active pseudo-classes can be used to specify explicit colors to indicate the interactive status of hyperlinks. The color specified to the :hover pseudo-class is applied when the link has focus, ready to be activated.

The color specified to the :active pseudo-class is applied when the user actually activates the link, usually by clicking the mouse button while the cursor hovers above the link.

It is important to recognize that the :link pseudo-class selects only those <a> anchor elements that include a href attribute, not fragment anchors that simply mark positions in a page.

link.html
(fragment)

 1   Create a HTML document containing an ordered list in which each item is an anchor element

```
<ol>
<li><a name = "top">Fragment anchor</a>
<li><a href = "http://been-there">Visited link</a>
<li><a href = "http://go-there">Unvisited link</a>
</ol>
```

2 Save the HTML document then create a linked style sheet containing a rule to set anchor colors and weight
a { color : blue ; font-weight : bold }

link.css

3 Next add style rules to specify hyperlink status colors
a:link { color : red }
a:visited { color : gray }

4 Now add style rules to specify hyperlink interactive colors
a:hover { color : green }
a:active { color : orange }

5 Save the style sheet alongside the HTML document then open the web page in a browser and activate the hyperlinks to see the specified color in each state

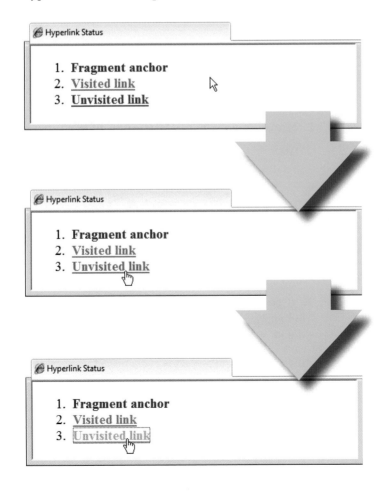

Hyperlink Status

1. **Fragment anchor**
2. **Visited link**
3. **Unvisited link**

Hyperlink Status

1. **Fragment anchor**
2. **Visited link**
3. **Unvisited link**

Hyperlink Status

1. **Fragment anchor**
2. **Visited link**
3. **Unvisited link**

Hot tip

Remember the difference between the pseudo-classes. Both **:link** and **:visited** apply static styles but **:hover**, **:active** (and **:focus**) apply styles dynamically in response to user actions.

121

Reacting to user events

User actions cause interface "events" to which the three dynamic pseudo-classes **:focus**, **:hover**, and **:active** can react. For example, when a user clicks on a text input the Focus event occurs – to which the **:focus** pseudo-class can react by applying styles.

Perhaps more interestingly, when the user moves the cursor onto any element the MouseOver event occurs – to which the **:hover** pseudo-class can react by applying styles. The applied styles are removed when the cursor moves off the element, as the MouseOut event occurs, creating a dynamic "rollover" effect.

Typically the rollover will highlight the selected element by changing its content color or background color to become more prominent. A rollover might also specify a different background image to create an image-swap – but this may not work too well on slower connections that need to wait for the new image to download.

A better image-swap alternative is to combine the images for both MouseOver and MouseOut states into a single image file, then have the rollover reveal the appropriate half of the image by specifying a different background position for each state.

rollover.png

1. Create an image file of 150x100 pixels containing two images, one above the other, on a transparent background

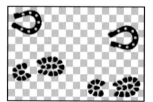

rollover.html
(fragment)

2. Next create a HTML document containing two empty "div" elements with id attributes for style rule reference
<div id = "box-1"></div>

   <div id = "box-2"></div>

3 Save the HTML document then create a linked style sheet with rules to set the div elements' absolute position and size – with a height exactly half that of the image

```
div#box-1 { position : absolute ; top : 10px ; left : 10px ;
                    width : 150px ; height : 50px }
div#box-2 { position : absolute ; top : 10px ; left: 170px ;
                    width : 150px ; height : 50px }
```

rollover.css

4 Now add style rules to color the backgrounds and set the background position at the top left corner of the image, when the cursor is not over the div elements

```
div#box-1 { background-color : blue }
div#box-2 { background : url(rollover.png) 0px 0px aqua }
```

5 Finally add style rules to change the background colors and set the background position at the center left of the image, when the cursor is over the div elements

```
div#box-1:hover { background-color : red }
div#box-2:hover {
              background : url(rollover.png) 0px -50px lime }
```

6 Save the style sheet alongside the HTML document then open the web page in a browser and roll the cursor over the div elements to see their backgrounds change

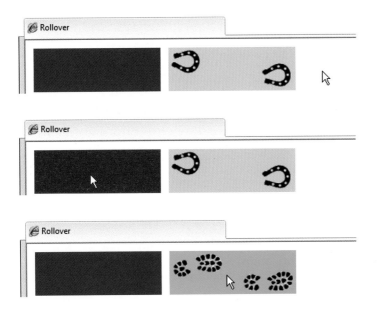

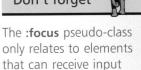

Don't forget

The **:focus** pseudo-class only relates to elements that can receive input – but the **:hover** pseudo-class relates to ANY element.

123

Interacting with CSS buttons

A rollover effect, as described in the previous example, can be combined with a hyperlink to create a navigation "button" using dynamic pseudo-classes to style hyperlink anchor elements. It is generally desirable to nest the anchor element within an outer containing element of defined size, then apply a rule setting the **display** property of the anchor element to **block** – so it expands up to the boundaries of the containing element. This makes the entire area of the containing element "clickable" and the anchor element's background will fill the container. A vertical column of navigation buttons can easily be created as a definition list in which each list item is a button.

buttons.html
(fragment)

buttons.css

1. Create a HTML document containing a definition list with a hyperlink in each list item

```
<dl id = "menu">
<dt class="btn"><a href = "a.html">Button 1</a></dt>
<dt class="btn"><a href = "b.html">Button 2</a></dt>
<dt class="btn"><a href = "c.html">Button 3</a></dt>
</dl>
```

2. Save the HTML document then create a linked style sheet containing a rule to set the list position and size

```
dl#menu { position : absolute ;
                top : 10px ; left : 20px ; width : 150px }
```

3. Next add a style rule to vertically space the list items and position their text content centrally

```
dt.btn { margin-bottom : 5px ; text-align : center }
```

4. Now add a style rule to expand the anchor elements to fill their containing list item content boxes, color the text, and suppress the default hyperlink underlines

```
dt.btn a { display : block ; color : white ;
                font-weight : bold ; text-decoration : none }
```

5. Finally add style rules to color the buttons differently according to the hyperlink status

```
dt.btn a:link, a:visited
            { background : blue ; border : 5px outset blue }
dt.btn a:hover
            { background : red ; border : 5px outset red }
dt.btn a:active
            { background : green ; border : 5px inset green }
```

6 Save the style sheet alongside the HTML document then open the web page in a browser to see the button appearance change in response to user actions

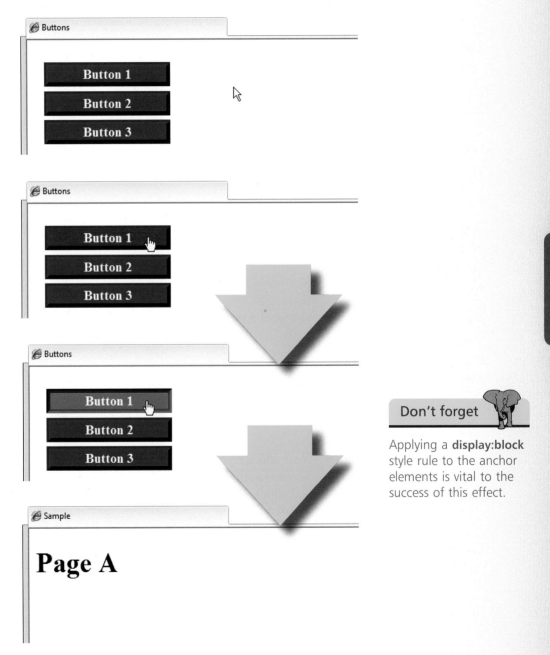

Don't forget

Applying a **display:block** style rule to the anchor elements is vital to the success of this effect.

Moving CSS tabs

In addition to changing the appearance of the selected element, to create a rollover effect, the three dynamic CSS pseudo-classes of **:focus, :hover,** and **:active** can apply styles that change the size or position of the selected element to create a further dynamic effect. For example, with absolutely positioned elements a style rule can specify different offset values to reposition the selected element in response to a user action.

Alternatively the element size can be dynamically changed by specifying different values to its **padding** property. This is often a better option and can be used to create slide-out hyperlink tabs.

tabs.html
(fragment)

tabs.css

1. Create a HTML document containing a definition list with a hyperlink in each list item
```
<dl id = "menu">
<dt class="tab"><a href="a.html">Tab 1</a></dt>
<dt class="tab"><a href="b.html">Tab 2</a></dt>
<dt class="tab"><a href="c.html">Tab 3</a></dt>
</dl>
```

2. Save the HTML document then create a linked style sheet containing a rule to set the list position and size
```
dl#menu { position : absolute ;
                      top : 0px ; left : 10px ; margin : 0 }
```

3. Next add a style rule to horizontally space the list items and position their text content centrally
```
dt.tab { display : block ; float : left ;
                margin-right : 5px ; text-align : center }
```

4. Now add a style rule to expand the anchor elements to fill their containing list item content boxes, color the text, and suppress the default hyperlink underlines
```
dt.tab a { display : block ; text-decoration : none ;
            color : white ; font-weight : bold ; width : 100px }
```

5. Finally add style rules to color the tabs differently and adjust their size according to the hyperlink status
```
dt.tab a { background : blue ; border : 5px outset blue }
dt.tab a:hover { padding-top :20px ; background : red ;
                                    border-color : red }
dt.tab a:active { padding-top : 20px ; background : green ;
                                    border-color : green }
```

6 Save the style sheet alongside the HTML document then open the web page in a browser to see the tab appearance and size change in response to user actions

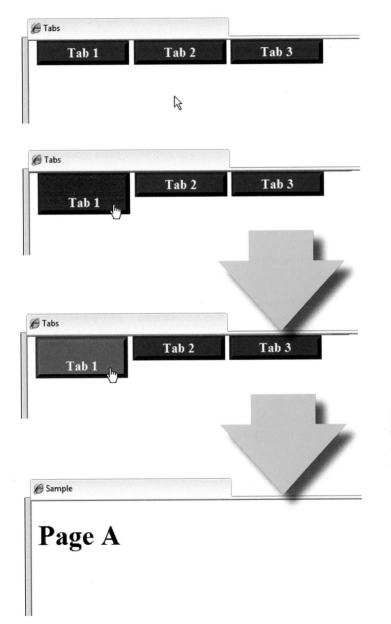

Beware

Use dynamic resizing with caution as it may hide other content unless all content is absolutely positioned to allow for resized content boxes.

Hiding & revealing elements

Besides the ability to style an element's appearance, position, and size, the three dynamic CSS pseudo-classes of :**focus**, :**hover**, and :**active** can control whether the selected element is even visible.

Specifying the **hidden** keyword to an element's **visibility** property will hide the element. Conversely a **hidden** element can be revealed by specifying the **visible** keyword to its **visibility** property.

Images placed on hidden elements that are absolutely positioned at the same coordinates can be revealed individually as the user places the cursor over scaled down "thumbnail" versions of each image – to produce a more compact page.

visibility.html
(fragment)

1. Create a HTML document containing a definition list with an anchor element in each item that encloses two image elements – one scaled down and one full size
```
<dl id = "pix">
<dt><a><img src = "65vette.jpg" width="66"
                          height="40" alt="65 Thumbnail">
<img class = "hid" src="65vette.jpg" width="250"
                height="150" alt="65 Vette"></a></dt>

<dt><a><img src = "67vette.jpg"  width="66"
                          height="40" alt="67 Thumbnail">
<img class = "hid" src="67vette.jpg" width="250"
                height="150" alt="67 Vette"></a></dt>
</dl>
```

visibility.css

2. Save the HTML document then create a linked style sheet containing rules to position the list
```
dl#pix   { position : absolute ; top : 10px ; left : 10px }
```

3. Next add a style rule to position and hide the image elements containing the full size images
```
dl#pix a img.hid { width : 250px ; height : 150px ; top : 0px ;
position : absolute ; left : 120px ; visibility : hidden }
```

4. Now add a style rule to reveal a full size image element when the cursor is placed over its scaled down version
```
dl#pix a:hover img.hid { visibility : visible }
```

5. Save the style sheet alongside the HTML document then open the web page in a browser and place the cursor over a scaled down image to see its full size version

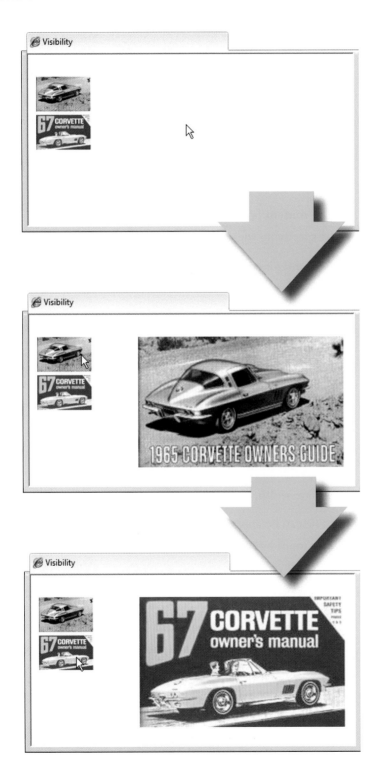

Don't forget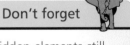

Hidden elements still occupy space in the document – they just can't be seen.

Summary

- CSS provides the four pseudo-elements :**before**, :**after**, :**first-letter**, and :**first-line**, that can enhance HTML content

- The **content** property can specify text content to generate, or quote marks with the **open-quote** and **close-quote** keywords

- Additionally non-text can be generated by specifying items within the parentheses of the **url()** or **attr()** keywords to the **content** property

- The **content** property may also generate automatic numbering by specifying the **counter()** keyword

- A **counter-increment** property can specify a counter name and increment value but may be reset by the **counter-reset** property

- The :**first-child** pseudo-class acts on the first selected element contained within an outer element

- Content languages can be identified by the :**lang()** pseudo-class

- The **cursor** property may specify a particular cursor to display using the cursor keywords or by stating the path to a cursor file within the parentheses of the **url()** keyword

- The **outline** property can specify the individual **outline-style**, **outline-width**, and **outline-color** properties as CSS shorthand

- Style can be applied to an interactive element that can receive user input by the :**focus** pseudo-class

- Hyperlink status can be indicated using the :**link**, :**visited**, :**hover**, and :**active** pseudo-classes

- Rollover effects with images, or on buttons and tabs, can also be achieved with :**link**, :**visited**, :**hover**, and :**active** pseudo-classes

- Setting the **display** property of an anchor element to **block** expands it to the boundaries of its containing element

- A selected element's **visibility** property may specify **hidden** or **visible** to determine whether its content should be displayed

8 Following guidelines

This chapter demonstrates established best practices that have been adopted by style sheet authors.

Resetting browser defaults

Cascading Style Sheets allow the web designer powerful control over every aspect of the page content but it must be remembered that each browser has default values that will be applied to elements in the absence of CSS style rules for those elements. This can cause inconsistencies in the appearance of the page design across different browsers so it is important to reset the browser's default values to ensure the style sheet has total control of the design so it will appear the same in different browsers.

A commonly-seen reset using the universal selector looks like this:

* { margin : 0 ; padding : 0 }

This rigorously resets the margin and padding areas to zero on every single element in the document but is not the best reset technique because it is heavy on the browser's rendering engine.

To reset the browser's default values the style rules should select each element to be reset and specify how they should be reset.

Hot tip

The reset style rules in this example are based upon the Yahoo! UI Library – further details can be found online at **http://developer.yahoo. com/yui/reset**.

reset.css

1 Create a reset style sheet with a rule to explicitly set element margin and padding areas to zero
body,div,dl,dt,dd,ul,ol,li,h1,h2,h3,h4,h5,h6,pre,form, fieldset,input,textarea,p,blockquote,th,td { margin : 0 ; padding : 0 }

2 Next add a style rule to collapse table element borders
table { border-collapse : collapse ; border-spacing : 0 }

3 Now add a style rule to set element borders to zero
fieldset,img,abbr,acronym { border : 0 }

4 Then add a style rule to set the font appearance
address,caption,cite,code,dfn,em,strong,th,var { font-style : normal ; font-weight : normal }

5 Now add a style rule to remove list markers
ol,ul { list-style : none }

6 Next add a style rule to left-align text content
caption,th,td { text-align : left }

7 Add a style rule to set the font appearance of headings
h1,h2,h3,h4,h5,h6
{ font-size : 100% ; font-weight : normal }

8 Finally add a style rule to add a space before and after quotation elements
q:before,q:after { content : " " }

9 Save the style sheet as "reset.css" for inclusion at the beginning of all your other style sheets to reset the browser default styles before other rules are applied

10 Create another style sheet that begins by resetting the browser's default style values
@import "reset.css" ;

neutral.css

11 Save the second style sheet alongside the first one then create a HTML document, linked to the second style sheet
<h1>Large Heading</h1><h3>Small Heading</h3>
<ol><li>One<li>Two<li>Three</ol>
<table><caption>Table</caption>
<tr><td>One</td><td>Two</td><td>Three</td></tr>
</table>

neutral.html
(fragment)

12 Save the HTML document alongside the style sheets then open the web page in a browser to see how the default browser styles have been removed

Default Styles

Large Heading

Small Heading

1. One
2. Two
3. Three

Table
One Two Three

Reset Styles

Large Heading
Small Heading
One
Two
Three
Table
OneTwoThree

133

Organizing your code

Modular style sheets

When styling large websites it is useful to make individual style sheets for different purposes and then link them in a single master style sheet. For example, maintain browser reset styles, typographic styles, and structure styles independently in different style sheets then link them together in a master style sheet, like this:

```
@import "reset.css" ;
@import "structure.css" ;
@import "typography.css" ;
```

Hot tip

The **@import** directive can optionally use the **url()** keyword, such as **@import url("reset.css");** but it's not essential.

Describing sections

Each style sheet should ideally be separated into sections with commented headings describing the purpose of that section. This makes the code easier for others to understand and easier for yourself to understand when revisiting the code some time later. For example, describing a navigation panel section:

```
/*********************************/

/* Primary Navigation - Top Links */

/*********************************/

div#nav {
border : 0.5em solid red ;
margin : 1em auto ;
padding : 0.2em
}
```

Code consistency

Some style sheet authors like to list the rule declarations in alphabetical property order to more readily find a declaration – like those listed in the code section above. Additionally it is good practice to omit the terminating semi-colon after the final declaration but some style sheet authors prefer to include it so further declarations can be simply appended at a later date. The general rule of thumb when writing style rules is to place the declarations on separate lines when there are more than three declarations, otherwise place them on a single line. Above all it is recommended you adopt your preferred style of writing style sheets and use it consistently.

1 Create a simple HTML document containing one heading and one paragraph
```
<h1>CSS Code</h1>
<p>Style sheets should be organized for readability!</p>
```

code.html (fragment)

2 Save the HTML document then create a linked style sheet beginning with a descriptive header
```
/*
Description: Tabloid newspaper format.
Author: Mike McGrath
Version: 1.0
*/
```

code.css

3 Next add a directive to reset the browser default styles
```
/* Reset browser defaults. */
@import "reset.css" ;
```

4 Now add a single-line rule for the paragraph content
```
/* Text content. */
p { font : large cursive  }
```

5 Finally add a multi-line alphabetically arranged rule for the heading element
```
/* Banner headings. */
h1 {
background : red ;
color : white ;
font : 2em white ;
padding: 0.2em ;
width : 5em }
```

Don't forget

Remember to add a terminating semi-colon after each **@import** directive.

6 Save the style sheet alongside the HTML document then open the web page in a browser to see the rules applied

135

Optimizing style rules

Inheriting values

In order to optimize style sheet code it's important to recognize that many property values of a parent element are inherited by the child element it contains. Most commonly the **font** and **color** properties are inherited from the containing parent element. So if a style rule sets these properties for the parent element a further rule need not repeat them for the child element – unless different values are desired. For example:

div { font-size : 2em ; color : red }
div.hello { font-size : 2em ; color : blue }

...can be written more efficiently as:

div { font-size : 2em ; color : red }
div.hello { color : blue }

Sizing text

When specifying text size it is best practice to avoid absolute unit values in order to allow the user to enlarge text. The preferred method is to size text relative to the browser using **em** units. Standard browser font size is **1em,** which is equal to **16px.** A little web designer trick is to reset the font size with this style rule:

body { font-size : 62.5% }

This sets **1em = 10px** so where, for example, an **18px** text size is desired a rule declaration of **font-size : 1.8em** can be specified without the need to calculate the **em** size.

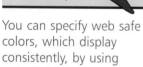
Employing shorthand

Always use CSS shorthand properties rather than individual properties to keep style sheet code concise. For example:

margin-left : 2px ;
margin-top : 3px ;
margin-right : 4px ;
margin-bottom : 5px ;

...can be written more efficiently as:

margin : 3px 4px 5px 2px ;

Similarly use shorthand for **border, background, padding, font** and other properties. Additionally, with color values represented by three pairs of hexadecimal digits its value can be specified more efficiently by omitting every second digit like this:

#ff3366 ...can be written as: **#f36.**

1 Create a HTML document with a single paragraph containing two sections of spanned text

```
<p>
Optimized text with <br><span>inherited values</span>
<br>and also <span id="mod">overriding values</span>
</p>
```

optimum.html
(fragment)

2 Save the HTML document then create a linked style sheet with a directive to reset the default browser styles

```
/* Reset browser defaults. */
@import "reset.css" ;
```

optimum.css

3 Next add a style rule to reset the font

```
/* Reset the font so that 1em=10px. */
body { font-size : 62.5% }
```

4 Now add a style rule to set text size and color

```
/* Set the text size to 18px and color. */
p { font-size : 1.8em ; color : red }
```

5 Then add a style rule to override an inherited value

```
/* Override inherited color value. */
span#mod { color : blue }
```

6 Finally add a style rule to set borders with shorthand

```
/* Set borders using shorthand. */
p { border : 3px dashed #0f0 }
```

7 Save the style sheet alongside the HTML document then open the web page in a browser to see the optimum styles

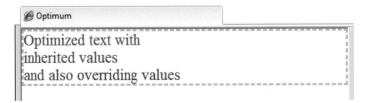

Employing multiple classes

A HTML element's **class** attribute can be assigned multiple values, each separated by a space. This is a very powerful feature of CSS, allowing you to apply styles from more than one class to any element.

classes.html
(fragment)

classes.css

1 Create a HTML document containing six paragraphs that each include a class attribute
```
<p class="bdr">Border Style</p>
<p class = "bdr mgn">Border + Margin Style</p>
<p class="bdr mgn txt">
                    Border + Margin + Text Style</p>
<p class="bdr mgn txt pad">
          Border + Margin + Text + Padding Style</p>
<p class="bdr mgn txt pad bg">
Border + Margin + Text + Padding + Background Style</p>
<p class="bdr mgn pad bg">
       Border + Margin + Padding + Background Style</p>
```

2 Save the HTML document then create a linked style sheet with a directive to reset the default browser styles
```
/* Reset browser defaults. */
@import "reset.css" ;
```

3 Next add a style rule for a border class
```
/* Border style. */
p.bdr { border : 5px outset red }
```

4 Now add a style rule for a margin class
```
/* Margin size. */
p.mgn { margin : 1em }
```

5 Then add a style rule for a text class
```
/* Text style. */
p.txt { font : 2em fantasy }
```

6 Now add a style rule for a padding class
```
/* Padding. */
p.pad { padding : 0.5em }
```

7 Finally add a style rule for a background class
```
/* Background. */
p.bg { background : yellow }
```

8 Save the style sheet alongside the HTML document then open the web page in a browser to see the various class styles applied to the paragraphs

 Multiple Classes

Border Style

Border + Margin Style

Border + Margin + Text Style

Border + Margin + Text + Padding Style

Border + Margin + Text + Padding + Background Style

Border + Margin + Padding + Background Style

Don't forget

Notice that the margin width increases when the text size is increased because the margin width value is specified as a relative **em** value.

139

Hot tip

Typically when using multiple classes each style rule will only define one or two properties.

Validating style sheets

Web browsers make no attempt to validate code so it's well worth verifying every HTML document and CSS style sheet before the web page is published, even when the page looks fine in your browser. When the browser encounters code errors it makes a guess at what is intended – but different browsers may make different interpretations and so display the page incorrectly. The World Wide Web Consortium (W3C) provide free online validator tools that check web page code for errors.

The W3C is the recognized body that oversees standards on the web. See the latest developments on their informative website at **www.w3.org**.

1 Create a HTML document and a linked CSS style sheet

2 With an Internet connection, open a web browser and navigate to the W3C HTML Validator Tool at **http://validator.w3.org** then click the "Validate by File Upload" tab and select your HTML document

3 Now click the "Check" button to upload a copy of your file then see the test result appear

Hot tip

Other tabs in the HTML Validator allow you to enter the web address of an online document to validate or copy'n'paste code for validation.

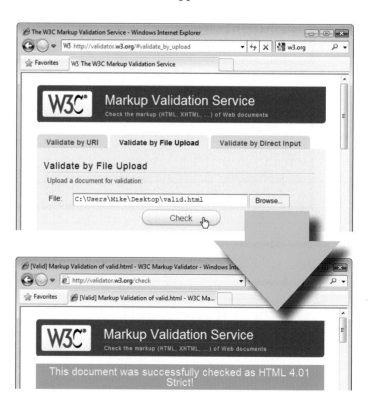

If validation fails the errors are listed so you may easily correct them. When validation succeeds you may choose to include a W3C HTML validation icon at the end of the HTML document

4. Next navigate to the W3C CSS Validator Tool at **http://jigsaw.w3.org/css-validator/** then click the "By file upload" tab and select your CSS style sheet

5. Now click the "Check" button to upload a copy of your file then see the test result appear

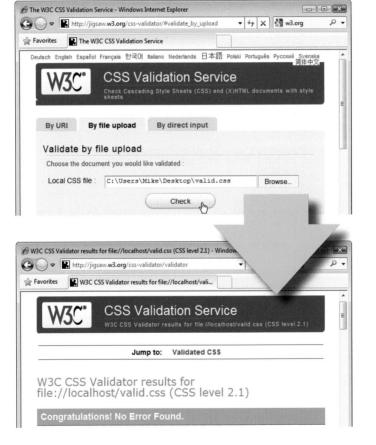

If validation fails the errors are listed so you may easily correct them. When validation succeeds you may choose to include a W3C CSS validation icon at the end of the HTML document

Compressing code files

Lengthy CSS style sheets can be streamlined for faster download time by "minification" to preserve the operational qualities of the code while reducing its overall byte footprint. The minification process removes comments, unnecessary whitespace, and line breaks.

One of the best minification tools is the YUI Compressor that is part of the Yahoo! UI Library and is freely available for download at **http://developer.yahoo.com/yui/compressor**. This application is written in Java, so requires Java version 1.4 or later to be installed on your computer.

1 With Java installed, download the YUI Compressor and place the **yuicompressor-x.x.x.jar** file on your desktop

2 Next copy the style sheet to be minified to your desktop, say the "reset.css" file described earlier

Hot tip

The YUI Compressor can also be used to minify JavaScript code files.

```
reset.css - Notepad
File  Edit  Format  View  Help
/*
Description: Browser Default Styles Reset.
Author: Mike McGrath
Version: 1.0
*/

/* Reset margin and padding areas. */
body,div,dl,dt,dd,ul,ol,li,h1,h2,h3,h4,h5,h6,pre,
form,fieldset,input,textarea,p,blockquote,th,td
{
  margin : 0 ; padding : 0
}

/* Turn off table borders. */
table {
border-collapse : collapse ; border-spacing : 0 }

/* Turn off other borders. */
fieldset,img,abbr,acronym {  border : 0 }

/* Set text to normal. */
address,caption,cite,code,dfn,em,strong,th,var {
font-style : normal ; font-weight : normal }
h1,h2,h3,h4,h5,h6 {
font-size : 100% ; font-weight : normal }

/* Turn off list markers. */
ol,ul { list-style : none }

/* Left align caption and cell text. */
caption,th,td { text-align : left }

/* Add a space around quotes. */
q:before,q:after { content : " " }
```

…cont'd

3 Insert a ! character after the opening /* of any comments you wish to keep, say the heading, then save the changes

4 Now open a Command Prompt window then use the **cd** command to navigate to your desktop

5 At the Command Prompt issue the following command to minify the style sheet and overwrite the existing file, replacing **x.x.x** with the version number of your download
java -jar yuicompressor-x.x.x.jar reset.css -o reset.css

Hot tip

The command in this example states the input and output files as the same name to overwrite the original file with the minified output but a different output file name could be used to preserve the original file.

6 When the operation completes, open the style sheet in a plain text editor to see the minified code with the heading comment preserved

```
/*!Description:Browser Default Styles Reset.
Author:Mike McGrath Version:1.0 */
body,div,dl,dt,dd,ul,ol,li,h1,h2,h3,h4,h5,h6,pre,fo
rm,fieldset,input,textarea,p,blockquote,th,td
{margin:0;padding:0;}table{border-
collapse:collapse;border-spacing:0;}
fieldset,img,abbr,acronym{border:0;}
address,caption,cite,code,dfn,em,strong,th,var
{font-style:normal;font-weight:normal;}
h1,h2,h3,h4,h5,h6{font-size:100%;font-
weight:normal;}ol,ul{list-style:none;}
caption,th,td{text-align:left;}q:before,q:after
{content:" ";}
```

Hot tip

Add a **-v** option before the input file name in the command to see verbose output from the YUI Compressor advising of any errors.

Comparing the file size of the original and minified versions of the style sheet in this example reduced the original from 833 bytes to 504 bytes – a saving of almost 40%. Of course this is just a small example but the savings can be considerable on larger, heavily commented, style sheet files.

143

Summary

- Default styles may vary between browsers so it is best to always reset the browser defaults to ensure the style sheet has control

- A browser reset should select each element to be reset and specify how they should be reset

- Modular style sheets can be created for different aspects of a website then incorporated in a single master style sheet

- Each style sheet should ideally be separated into sections with commented headings describing the purpose of that section

- Style rule declarations can be listed in alphabetical property order to readily find any declaration

- You may omit the terminating semi-colon after the final declaration in a style rule as it is superfluous

- Place style rules with fewer than four declarations on a single line, otherwise place them on multiple lines

- Do not repeatedly specify style rules for property values inherited from a parent element

- Avoid absolute units when specifying text size and use relative **em** units instead so the user can enlarge text

- Always use CSS shorthand properties rather than individual properties to keep style sheet code concise

- Multiple classes can be assigned to a HTML element's **class** attribute to apply styles from more than one CSS class

- All HTML documents and CSS style sheets can be validated by the W3C online validation tools

- Style sheet file sizes can be reduced by minification to remove comments, unnecessary whitespace, and line breaks

9 Customizing pages

This chapter demonstrates how to apply multiple style sheets to a single web page for user choice and to suit different devices.

Recognizing media

CSS can provide different style sheets to allow the user to choose a preferred layout style and produce layouts appropriate for various situations. Adding a **media** attribute to the HTML **<link>** tag can specify a style sheet to be used for all devices with the **all** keyword, or specify style sheets for viewing on computer screens with the **screen** keyword. Other style sheets can be specified for mobile devices, such as cellphones, with the **handheld** keyword. Additionally, a style sheet for printer output can be specified with the **print** keyword, which will typically remove navigation links and advertizing.

custom.html
(fragment)

Hot tip

Notice that alternative style sheets for viewing this web page on a computer screen are specified by assigning a value of "alternate stylesheet" to the HTML **rel** attribute.

1 Create a HTML document that specifies a variety of style sheets in its head section

```
<link rel="stylesheet" type="text/css" media="screen"
                    href="screen.css" title="Default Style">
<link rel="alternate stylesheet" type="text/css"
media="screen" href="reverse.css"
                              title="Reverse Color Style">
<link rel="alternate stylesheet" type="text/css"
media="screen" href="large.css" title="Large Text Style">
<link rel="alternate stylesheet" type="text/css"
media="screen" href="legacy.css" title="Simple Text Style">
<link rel="stylesheet" type="text/css" media="handheld"
         href="handheld.css" title="Mobile Device Style">
<link rel="stylesheet" type="text/css" media="print"
                    href="print.css" title="Printer Style">
```

2 Now add content within "div" elements in the body section

```
<div id="wrapper">
<div id="head"><h1>Cascading Style Sheets...</h1>
</div><div id="list">
<ul><li>Screen<li>Reverse<li>Large<li>Legacy
<li>Handheld<li>Print</ul></div>
<div id="tips"><h3>W3C</h3>The World Wide Web
Consortium oversees web standards.
<h3>XSL</h3>The eXtensible Stylesheet Language is less
popular than CSS.</div>
<div id="content"><h2>What is CSS?</h2>Cascading
Style Sheets are used to control the presentational aspects
of HTML documents. It was created by the World Wide
Web consortium to regain control of document markup.
Websites designed with external CSS style sheets are more
easily maintained than those using internal style sheets as
the style code is centralized. CSS reduces website file sizes
for faster downloading and provides precision control over
web page presentation.</div></div>
<div id="foot">Styled by CSS in easy steps</div>
```

...cont'd

3 Save the HTML document then open the web page in a browser to see how the content appears with the web browser's default styles

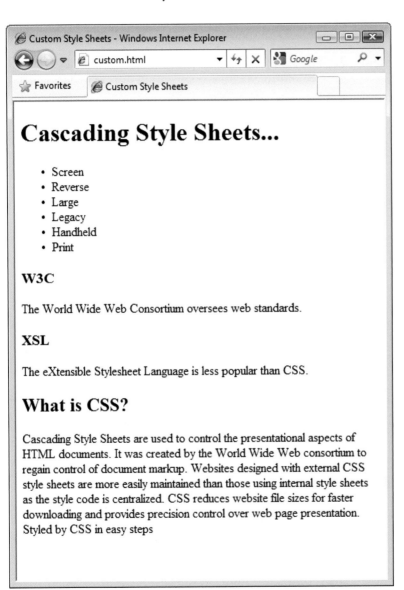

Don't forget

Style sheets to format this basic HTML document are described throughout the rest of this chapter.

147

Adding page structure

The simple HTML document created on the previous page can be structured in several ways by CSS style sheets. Typically regular web browsers can present its content as a familiar 3-column layout with a header and footer area, as described on page 70. Browser default styles should first be reset, as described on page 132.

screen.css

structure.css

1 Create a linked style sheet for the HTML document created on the previous page with a directive to initially reset the default browser styles
@import "reset.css";

2 Next add another directive to execute style rules that structure the HTML document's elements
@import "structure.css";

3 Save the style sheet alongside the HTML document then create a new style sheet with rules to ensure the document occupies the full height of the browser window
html, body { height : 100% }

div#wrapper {
min-height : 100% ;
height : auto !important ;
margin : 0 auto -30px
}

4 Now add style rules to set the height of the header and footer areas
div#head { height : 60px }
div#foot { height : 30px }

5 Then add style rules to specify the column sizes
div#list { float : left ; width : 100px ; margin-left : 1.5em }
div#tips { float : right ; width : 100px }
div#content { margin : 0 120px }

6 Save the style sheet alongside the HTML document then open the web page in a browser to see the content appear in a 3-column structure with a header and footer area

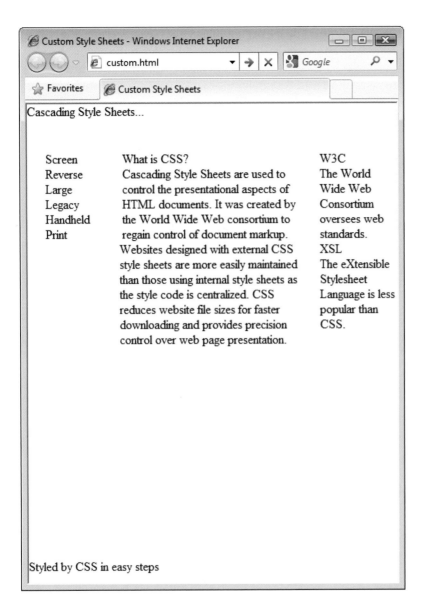

Hot tip

The browser knows to use these style sheets in a web browser because it recognizes the media as "screen" from the **media** attribute in the **<link>** element.

Specifying default styles

The structured HTML document content described on the previous page can be stylized by adding rules to the default style sheet used by the browser for the screen media. If necessary the style sheet can be explicitly selected by choosing the name assigned to the **title** attribute in the **<link>** tag. In this example the name given is simply "Default Style".

screen.css

1 Edit the style sheet from the previous page by adding a rule to specify the overall background and text color
body { background : url(drops.jpg) white ; color : black }

2 Now add style rules to determine the appearance of each heading element
h1 { font : 2em sans-serif ; color : red }
h2 { color : blue ;
font : 1.2em "Lucida Handwriting", cursive }
h3 { background : red ; color : white }

3 Next add a style rule to specify how the list markers should appear
ul { list-style : url(tick.png) square ; margin-left : 10px }

4 Then add a style rule to set the font for text within the main content area
div#content { font : 1em sans-serif }

5 Finally add a style rule to determine how the footer area should appear
div#foot {
text-align : center; background : blue ; color : white }

6 Save the style sheet alongside the HTML document then open the web page in a browser to see the structured document appear with color, image, and font styles

7 Open the browser's style sheet dialog (with Internet Explorer click View, Style on the menu bar) and note that the name assigned to the **<link>** element's **title** attribute is currently selected

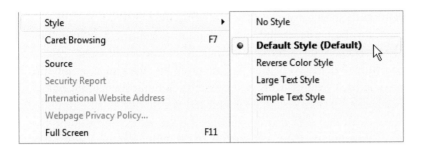

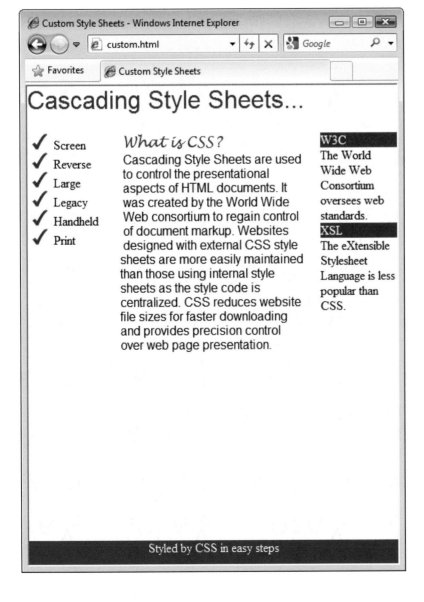

Don't forget

Always specify an alternative style in case images are not available – here the alternatives are a white background and square list markers.

Specifying reverse styles

Alternate styling for the default styling described on the previous page can be made available to the user by creating another style sheet specified as "alternate stylesheet" to the **<link>** tag's **rel** attribute. Mostly web page styling employs black text on a white or pale background as it resembles the familiar format found in books and magazines. A high colored alternative can be provided using white or pale text on a colored background – reversing the typical format. To apply alternate styling the user simply chooses the name assigned to the **<link>** element's **title** attribute from the browser's style sheet dialog.

reverse.css

1. Create a new style sheet with directives to once again reset the browser's default styling and structure the content in a 3-column layout with header and footer areas
@import "reset.css" ;
@import "structure.css" ;

2. Next add a style rule to determine the overall background and text color
body { background : blue ; color : white }

3. Now add style rules to determine the appearance of each heading element
h1 { font : 2em sans-serif ; color : aqua }
h2 { color : aqua ;
               font : 1.2em "Lucida Handwriting", cursive }
h3 { background : aqua ; color : black }

4. Next add a style rule to specify how the list markers should appear
ul { list-style : square ; margin-left : 10px }

5. Then add a style rule to set the font for text within the main content area and footer area
div#content { font : 1em sans-serif }
div#foot { text-align : center ;
               background : aqua ; color : black }

6. Save the style sheet alongside the HTML document then open the web page in a browser and select the alternate style sheet name in the dialog to apply the reverse styles

...cont'd

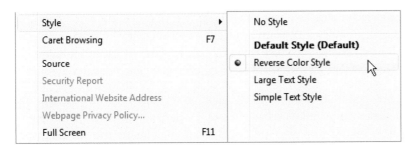

Style	▶	No Style
Caret Browsing	F7	**Default Style (Default)**
		Reverse Color Style
Source		Large Text Style
Security Report		Simple Text Style
International Website Address		
Webpage Privacy Policy...		
Full Screen	F11	

Beware

Avoid colored backgrounds for pages that the user is likely to print out – unless a separate printer style sheet is specified, as described on page 160.

153

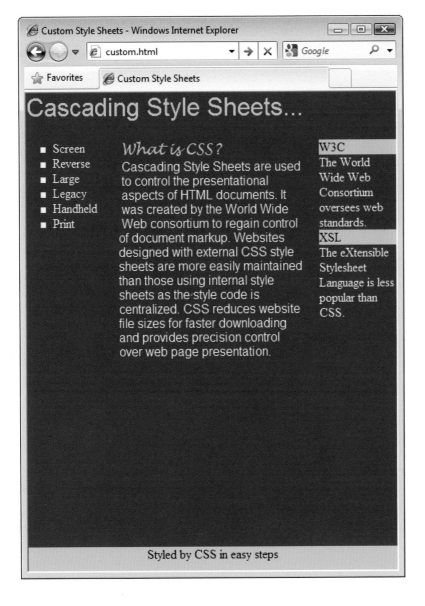

Custom Style Sheets - Windows Internet Explorer

custom.html   Google

☆ Favorites   Custom Style Sheets

Cascading Style Sheets...

- Screen
- Reverse
- Large
- Legacy
- Handheld
- Print

What is CSS?

Cascading Style Sheets are used to control the presentational aspects of HTML documents. It was created by the World Wide Web consortium to regain control of document markup. Websites designed with external CSS style sheets are more easily maintained than those using internal style sheets as the style code is centralized. CSS reduces website file sizes for faster downloading and provides precision control over web page presentation.

W3C
The World Wide Web Consortium oversees web standards.

XSL
The eXtensible Stylesheet Language is less popular than CSS.

Styled by CSS in easy steps

Improving readability

Another alternative layout to those described on the previous pages provides a version especially for low-vision (partially-sighted) users. Typically this will feature larger text and a linear layout where elements are stacked on top of each other vertically.

Headings may have inverted colors and often content will employ yellow text on a black background as partially-sighted people find these easiest to read. Additionally, some elements may be removed to clarify the page content.

large.css

1 Create a new style sheet with a directive to once again reset the browser's default styling
@import "reset.css" ;

2 Next add a style rule to determine the overall background, text size and color
body { font : bold large sans-serif ;
background : black ; color : yellow }

3 Now add a style rule to determine the appearance of each heading element
h1, h2, h3 { background : yellow ; color : black }

4 Finally add style rules to generate parentheses around the footer text
div#foot:before { content : "(" }
div#foot:after { content : ")" }

5 Save the style sheet alongside the HTML document then open the web page in a browser and select the alternate style sheet name in the dialog to apply low-vision styles

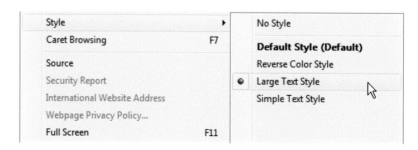

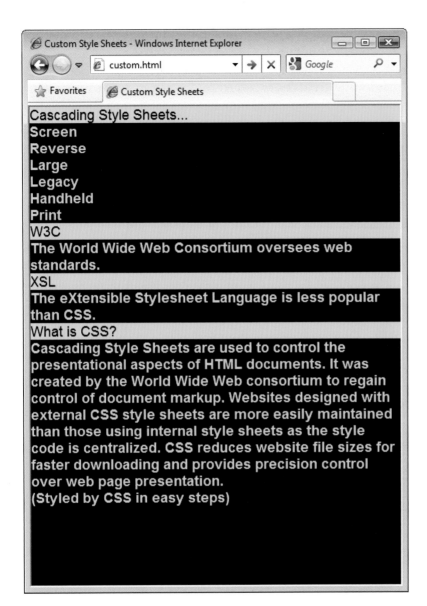

155

Hot tip

Other popular colors for low-vision web pages are white text on a navy background.

Reverting to legacy styles

The examples in this book demonstrate Cascading Style Sheets, level 2, which built upon Cascading Style Sheets, level 1 – so style sheets created for CSS1 also work in browsers that support CSS2. Additionally, style sheets created for CSS2 can be loaded in an older "legacy" browser that only supports CSS1 and the browser will ignore the elements and properties that it doesn't recognize.

There are some interesting differences between CSS1 and CSS2 – positioning in CSS2 is more flexible and offers more options to the designer. Automated content allows developers to force the browser to display specific content elements as well as control the layout, look, and feel. Also there is support for special cursors and dynamic outlining in CSS2.

An alternate style sheet to those described on the previous pages can be provided for those users with older legacy browsers that only support CSS1.

legacy.css

1   Create a new style sheet with a rule to determine the generic text font style
    body { font-family : sans-serif }

2   Now add style rules to determine the color of each heading element
    h1 { color : red }
    h2 { color : green }
    h3 { color : blue }

3   Save the style sheet alongside the HTML document then open the web page in a browser and select the alternate style sheet name in the dialog to apply CSS1 styles

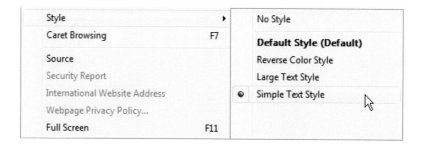

Don't forget

Legacy browsers may not support the **@import** directive so the browser reset is omitted here.

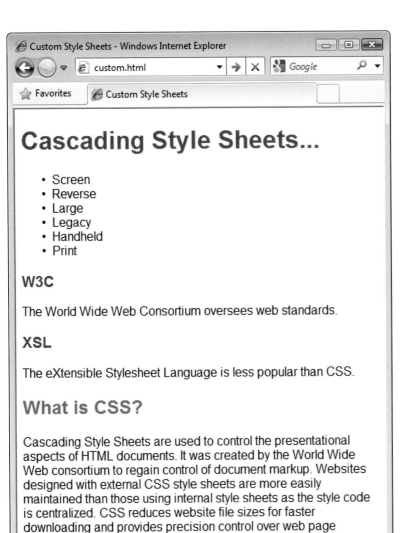

Cascading Style Sheets...

- Screen
- Reverse
- Large
- Legacy
- Handheld
- Print

W3C

The World Wide Web Consortium oversees web standards.

XSL

The eXtensible Stylesheet Language is less popular than CSS.

What is CSS?

Cascading Style Sheets are used to control the presentational aspects of HTML documents. It was created by the World Wide Web consortium to regain control of document markup. Websites designed with external CSS style sheets are more easily maintained than those using internal style sheets as the style code is centralized. CSS reduces website file sizes for faster downloading and provides precision control over web page presentation.
Styled by CSS in easy steps

Hot tip

Differences between CSS1 and CSS2 can be found on the W3C website at **www.w3.org/TR/REC-CSS2/changes.html**.

157

Providing handheld styles

Besides providing a variety of style sheets for viewing a page on a computer screen a style sheet can be created to determine how the page should appear on a handheld device, such as a cellphone.

For handheld devices the **<link>** element's **media** attribute should be assigned the **handheld** keyword, and its **title** attribute omitted.

When designing page layouts for viewing on handheld devices consideration should be given to the device limitations. For example, multi-column layouts should be avoided due to the tiny screens on handheld devices (typically 100-320 pixels wide), in favor of a single-column layout. Also unneccesary information should be suppressed to speed page load times – especially the removal of advertizing and images.

The clean simple layout suited to handheld devices is often also suitable for projected presentations, which can be identified by assigning the **projection** keyword to the **<link>** element's **media** attribute. Additionally multiple types can be assigned to this attribute as a comma-separated list, so the same style sheet can be specified for both handheld devices and projection with the attribute **media="handheld , projection"**.

handheld.css

1. Create a new style sheet with a directive to once again reset the browser's default styling
@import "reset.css" ;

2. Next add a style rule to specify the background and color of headings – to differentiate them from content text without using large fonts
h2 { background : red ; color : white }

3. Now add style rules to suppress unneccesary information – leaving just the actual content and its heading
div#list, div#foot, div#tips, h1, h3 { display : none }

4. Save the style sheet alongside the HTML document then open the web page in a browser on a handheld device, or via a projector, to see the simplified document

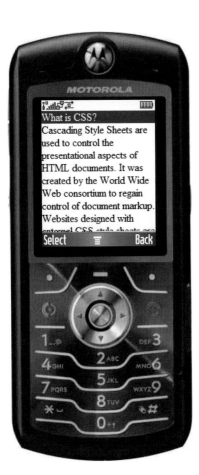

What is CSS?
Cascading Style Sheets are used to control the presentational aspects of HTML documents. It was created by the World Wide Web consortium to regain control of document markup. Websites designed with external CSS style sheets are

Scroll

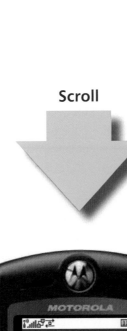

What is CSS?
external CSS style sheets are more easily maintained than those using internal style sheets as the style code is centralized. CSS reduces website file sizes for faster downloading and provides precision control over web page presentation.

Beware

Handheld devices often display content inconsistently – tables and CSS positioning are particularly troublesome.

Don't forget

With this example the browser retains the heading at the top of the screen when the user scrolls down the content.

Setting printer styles

Just as it is desirable to suppress some page items for display on handheld devices, as demonstrated in the previous example, it is often desirable to suppress items when printing pages.

For the printed page the **<link>** element's **media** attribute should be assigned the **print** keyword, and its **title** attribute omitted.

Where a color print is not required all color style rules can be removed in the print style sheet and prominence given to fonts.

When a print style sheet is defined the web browser will continue to display the page using the screen style sheet but will apply the print style sheet rules when sending the page to the printer. The print version can be seen with the browser's print preview feature.

print.css

1. Create a new style sheet with a rule to specify a uniform monospace font
body { font-family : monospace }

2. Now add a style rule to suppress unneccesary information – leaving just content and headings
div#foot, div#list { display : none }

3. Save the style sheet alongside the HTML document then open the web page in a browser and open the Print Preview to see the print style sheet rules get applied

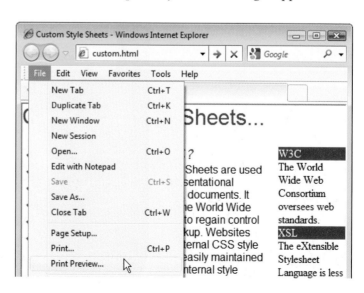

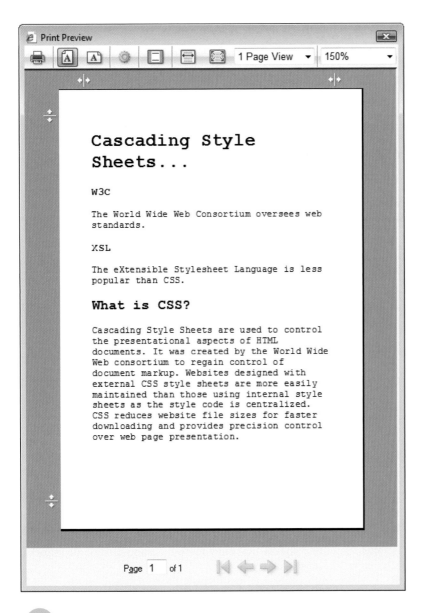

Don't forget

Always provide a print media style sheet to make a web page more user-friendly – with colors, unnecessary images and advertizing removed or suppressed.

4 Finally select File, Print on the browser menu to send the page to your printer and see the print appear with the print style rules applied

Summary

- CSS can provide different style sheets that allow the user to choose a preferred style and layout for various situations

- The HTML **<link>** element can include a **media** attribute that can be assigned the **all** keyword to specify a style sheet to be used for all devices

- Specifying a **screen** value to the **media** attribute designates a style sheet to be used only when viewed on a computer screen

- An **@import** directive can be used to include browser reset and layout structure style sheets within a master style sheet

- The HTML **<link>** element can include a **title** attribute with an assigned name that the user can select to use that style sheet

- Assigning a value of "alternate stylesheet" to the HTML **<link>** tag's **rel** attribute allows alternative style sheets to be specified for viewing on a computer screen

- The default style sheet will typically produce black content on a white background but a popular alternative style sheet will reverse this to produce white content on a dark background

- Style sheets for low-vision users typically arrange the content in a single-column layout with larger yellow text on a black background, as partially-sighted people find this easiest to read

- Old legacy browsers that only support CSS1 will display parts of CSS2 style sheets that they recognize and ignore all others

- Positioning in CSS1 is less flexible than in CSS2 so an alternative style sheet can be provided for legacy browsers

- Specifying a **handheld** value to the **media** attribute designates a style sheet to be used when viewed on a mobile device

- Specifying a **print** value to the **media** attribute designates a style sheet to be used when the page gets printed, and its appearance can be viewed in the browser's Print Preview

10 Looking ahead

This chapter demonstrates forthcoming CSS features that are already supported in some web browsers.

Rounding corners

The ability to round the corners of content box backgrounds and borders is at last provided by the **border-radius** property in the CSS 3.0 specifications. At the time of writing there are two different implementations of this feature.

For Mozilla applications, such as Firefox, the **-moz-border-radius** property is a shorthand for individual **-moz-border-radius-topleft**, **-moz-border-radius-topright**, **-moz-border-radius-bottomleft**, and **-moz-border-radius-bottomright** properties. These accept single length unit values to specify each radius and additionally extend the specification to allow percentage values. Specifying a single value to **-moz-border-radius** applies that radius to all four corners. Specifying two values applies the first to the top left and bottom right, and the second to both other corners. Specifying three values applies the first to the top left, the second to top right and bottom left, and the third to the bottom right corner. Specifying four values applies the values clockwise starting at the top left.

For the Safari and Google Chrome browsers the **-webkit-border-radius** property accepts either a single length unit value to specify a regular radius to apply to all four corners or two length unit values to specify an irregular radius to apply to all four corners. Similarly one or two length values can be specified to individual **-webkit-border-top-left-radius**, **-webkit-border-top-right-radius**, **-webkit-border-bottom-left-radius**, and **-webkit-border-bottom-right-radius** properties to set the radius of individual corners. Percentage values are not allowed though.

The differences between these two sets of properties are simply different interpretation of the specification. Currently to have rounded corners appear the same in Firefox, Safari, and Google Chrome only regular radii should be specified and percentage values avoided.

It should be noted that only corners of the background and border get rounded but the content box remains rectangular – so text content within the box begins by default in the top left corner of the rectangle as usual. This means that expanding a hyperlink element with a **display:block** rule to fill its containing element will fill the invisible rectangle – so the link may also be activated outside the rounded corner of the containing elements background where it remains inside the boundaries of the rectangular content box.

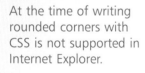

Don't forget

At the time of writing rounded corners with CSS is not supported in Internet Explorer.

1 Create a HTML document containing three "div" elements with a hyperlink in the third one
```
<div class="round">All Round Corners</div>
<div class="indie">Individual Round Corners</div>
<div class="ball">
        <a href="http://www.google.com">Ball</a></div>
```

corners.html
(fragment)

2 Save the HTML document then create a linked style sheet with a rule that positions the elements horizontally
```
div { float : left ; height : 100px ; margin : 10px ; color : #ff0 ;
width : 100px ; padding : 15px ; font : bold 1.2em cursive }
```

corners.css

3 Now add a style rule to round all corners of the first div
```
div.round { background-color : #f00 ;
 -moz-border-radius : 50px ; -webkit-border-radius : 50px }
```

4 Add a style rule to round two corners of the second div
```
div.indie { background-color : #080 ;
-moz-border-radius-topleft : 50px ;
-moz-border-radius-bottomleft : 50px ;
-webkit-border-top-left-radius : 50px ;
-webkit-border-bottom-left-radius : 50px }
```

165

5 Finally add style rules to create a circular background and border enclosing an expanded hyperlink element
```
div.ball { background-color : #00f ; height : 120px ;
width : 120px ; padding : 0 ; border : 5px solid navy ;
text-align : center ; -moz-border-radius : 65px ;
-webkit-border-radius : 65px }
a { color : aqua ; display : block ; height : 100% }
```

Hot tip

Padding is added to the first two elements to position the text inside the background.

6 Save the style sheet alongside the HTML element then open the web page in a browser to see rounded corners

Reducing opacity

The ability to reduce the opacity of content boxes is provided in the CSS 3.0 specifications with the introduction of an **opacity** property. This specifies the opacity as a numeric value in the range 0.0 - 1 where one is fully opaque and zero is fully transparent. For example, specifying a value of 0.5 will produce 50% opacity.

Additionally, opacity can be specified via the alpha channel following the introduction of RGBA notation using the new **rgba()** keyword. This specifies red, green, and blue, component values in the range 0 -255 as a comma-separated list (like the **rgb()** keyword described on page 48) and also an opacity value in the range 0.0 - 1 where one is fully opaque and zero is fully transparent. For example, specifying a value of **rgba(255,0,0,0.5)** will produce red at 50% opacity.

The key difference between these two methods of setting opacity is this:

- **The opacity property** – sets the opacity value for an element and all of its child content

- **The rgba() keyword** – sets the opacity value only for a single specific property

This means that text within a content box will inherit the opacity value when the **background** specifies a value to its **opacity** property. Conversely, text within a content box will not inherit the opacity value when the **background** specifies a value using the **rgba()** keyword.

In practice setting opacity with the **rgba()** keyword is most often desirable as it allows background opacity to be reduced while text content remains unaffected.

Don't forget

At the time of writing opacity with valid CSS is not supported in Internet Explorer, which instead supports a proprietary alternative such as **filter:alpha(opacity=50)**.

opacity.html
(fragment)

1. Create a HTML document containing four "div" elements with separate identities
```
<div id="bg1"></div>
<div id="fg1">50% Opacity</div>

<div id="bg2"></div>
<div id="fg2">50% Opacity</div>
```

...cont'd

2 Save the HTML document then create a linked style sheet with a rule that specifies the positioning scheme, size, and text styles for each div element
div { position : absolute ; height: 100px ; width : 100px ; font : bold 1.5em cursive ; color : #fff }

opacity.css

3 Next add a style rule that positions the first div element and sets its color
div#bg1 { top : 20px ; left : 20px ; background : rgb(255,255,0) ; z-index : 1 }

4 Now add a style rule that positions the second div element so it overlaps the first and sets its opacity to 50%
div#fg1 { top : 50px ; left : 50px ; background : rgb(0,0,255) ; opacity : 0.5; z-index : 2 }

5 Then add a style rule that positions the third div element and sets its color
div#bg2 { top : 20px ; left : 170px ; background : rgb(255,255,0) ; z-index : 1 }

6 Finally add a style rule that positions the fourth div element so it overlaps the third and sets its alpha to 50%
div#fg2 { top : 50px ; left : 200px ; background : rgba(0,0,255,0.5) ; z-index : 2 }

7 Save the style sheet alongside the HTML document then open the web page in a browser to see how the overlapping elements' text inherit colors differently

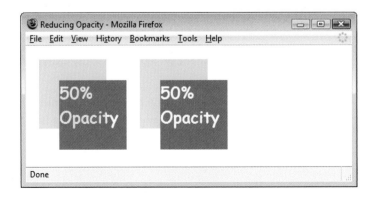

167

Don't forget

Notice that the z-index property, introduced on page 60, is used here to specify the elements' stacking order.

Adding shadows

The ability to add a drop shadow effect to content boxes is provided in the CSS 3.0 specifications with the introduction of the **box-shadow** property. This property takes three length values and a color value to specify how the drop shadow should appear. The length values specify these three features:

- **Horizontal offset** – a positive value places the shadow to the right of the content box and a negative value places it to its left

- **Vertical offset** – a positive value places the shadow below the content box and a negative value places it above the box

- **Blur radius** – zero sets the shadow to sharp, whereas the higher the number the more blurred the shadow will be

Where the content box background is given rounded corners by the **border-radius** property the drop shadow will follow the contour of the rounded corner.

At the time of writing there are two different implementations of the **box-shadow** property.

For Mozilla applications, such as Firefox, the **-moz-box-shadow** property takes the values described above but may also specify a further value with the **inset** keyword, which applies the shadow inside the content box rather than outside as usual.

For the Safari and Google Chrome browsers the **-webkit-box-shadow** property simply requires the values described above so the shadow cannot be specified inside the box.

shadow.html
(fragment)

shadow.css

1. Create a HTML document containing three "div" elements with different class attribute values
```
<div class="red-shadow">Drop Shadow</div>
<div class="green-shadow">Drop Shadow</div>
<div class="blue-shadow">Drop Shadow</div>
```

2. Save the HTML document then create a linked style sheet with a rule that positions the elements horizontally
```
div {
float : left ; height : 100px ; margin : 20px ; width : 100px ;
background : #fff ; border : 1px solid #000 }
```

3 Next add a style rule to create a red drop shadow for the first element
```
div.red-shadow {
-moz-box-shadow : 3px 5px 10px #f00 ;
-webkit-box-shadow : 3px 5px 10px #f00 }
```

4 Now add a style rule to create a green shadow on the second element, inset on Mozilla browsers only
```
div.green-shadow {
-moz-box-shadow :-3px -5px 10px #0f0 inset ;
-webkit-box-shadow : 3px 5px 10px #0f0 }
```

5 Finally add a style rule to create a blue shadow on the third element, following the contour of a rounded corner
```
div.blue-shadow {
-moz-border-radius-bottomright : 50px ;
-moz-box-shadow : 3px 5px 10px #00f ;
-webkit-border-bottom-right-radius : 50px ;
-webkit-box-shadow : 3px 5px 10px #00f }
```

6 Save the style sheet alongside the HTML document then open the web page in browsers to see the shadow effects

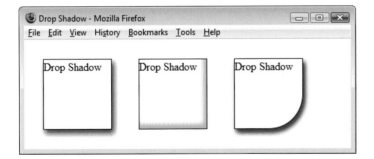

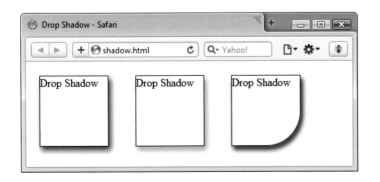

Don't forget

At the time of writing the CSS **box-shadow** property is not supported in Internet Explorer.

Hot tip

Avoid using the **inset** keyword so the shadow style will be displayed consistently across different browsers.

Creating resizable containers

The ability to allow content boxes to be dynamically resized by the user is provided in the CSS 3.0 specifications with the introduction of the **resize** property. This can specify that the content box can be resized both horizontally and vertically with the **both** keyword.

Typically a content box that can be resized will contain content that overflows the content box boundaries so its **overflow** property will need to determine how to handle the overflowing content. Specifying an **auto** value will automatically add scroll bars and indicate that the box may be resized by including a grab handle in its bottom right corner. Alternatively the scroll bars can be prohibited by specifying a **hidden** value – but the user then gets no visual clue that the box may be resized.

When allowing the user to resize a content box it is also useful to specify its maximum possible dimensions to limit how much the layout can be affected. Normally these will be specified as unit length values to the content box's **max-width** and **max-height** properties, matching the overall size of the content.

resize.html
(fragment)

1 Create a HTML document containing three "div" elements, with two containing images
```
<div class="nobars max">
<img src="image.jpg" alt="Squares"
                         width="150" height="150"></div>

<div class="bars max">
<img src="image.jpg" alt="Squares"
                         width="150" height="150"></div>
<div></div>
```

resize.css

2 Save the HTML document then create a linked style sheet with a rule that positions the elements horizontally
```
div {
float: left ; margin : 10px ; height : 75px ; width : 75px ;
background : #f00 ; border : 1px solid #000 }
```

3 Next add a style rule to allow the first element to be resized but provide no scroll bars
```
div.nobars
{ resize : both ; overflow : hidden }
```

4 Now add a style rule to allow the second element to be resized and do provide scroll bars
div.bars
{ resize : both ; overflow : auto }

5 Finally add a style rule to limit the extent to which the first two elements may be resized
div.max { max-height : 150px ; max-width : 150px }

6 Save the style sheet alongside the HTML document then open the web page in a browser and drag the bottom right corner of the first two elements to resize them

Beware

Notice that the scroll bars appear within the second element's boundaries – obscuring part of the image.

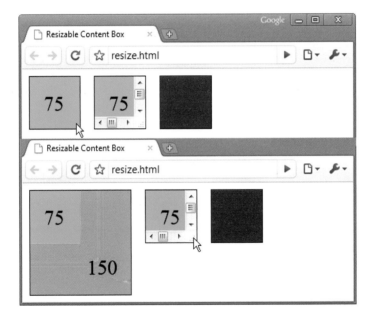

Hot tip

After resizing a content box the default layout scheme automatically repositions following elements – compare the positions of the red element in this example.

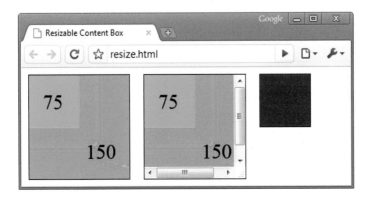

Summary

- The CSS 3.0 **border-radius** property provides the ability to round the background and border of content boxes

- Mozilla applications implement **border-radius** with the **-moz-border-radius** property that is shorthand for **-moz-border-radius-topleft, -moz-border-radius-topright, -moz-border-radius-bottomleft, -moz-border-radius-bottomright**

- Google Chrome and Safari browsers implement **border-radius** with the **-webkit-border-radius** property that can specify regular radii of four corners with a single length value, or irregular radii of four corners with two length values

- Regular or irregular radii can be specified for single corners using individual properties like **-webkit-border-top-left-radius**

- The CSS 3.0 **opacity** property provides the ability to specify transparency values of content within the range 0.0 - 1

- Alpha channel transparency set with the **rgba()** keyword only affects a single specific property, not child content

- The CSS 3.0 **box-shadow** property provides the ability to place a drop shadow effect around a content box by specifying a horizontal and vertical offset, blur radius, and color

- Mozilla applications implement **box-shadow** with the **-moz-box-shadow** property, whereas Google Chrome and Safari browsers use the **-webkit-box-shadow** property

- The **-moz-box-shadow** property extends the specification by allowing an **inset** keyword to place the shadow inside the box

- Drop shadows will follow the contour of rounded corners specified by the appropriate **border-radius** property

- The CSS 3.0 **resize** property provides the ability to allow the user to dynamically resize a content box both vertically and horizontally when it specifies the **both** keyword

Reference section

This section of the book lists all the established visual CSS properties and values.

Properties and values

The tables in this section list by Name each visual CSS property and their possible Values.

Each CSS property can be applied to any HTML element unless specific target elements are given in the table. For instance, a **border-collapse** property can only be applied to table and inline-table elements, whereas a **background** property can be applied to any element.

Similarly, properties are not inherited unless specifically marked as ^Inherited. For instance, the **border-collapse** property is inherited but the background property is not.

In each case the Initial Value is the default value that will be inferred unless a valid alternative value is explicitly specified in a style rule.

Name	Values	Initial Value
background	[*background-color*		*background-image*		*background-repeat*		*background-attachment*		*background-position*]	**inherit**	see individual properties
background-attachment	**scroll**	**fixed**	**inherit**	scroll
background-color	*color*	**transparent**	**inherit**	transparent
background-image	*url*	**none**	**inherit**	none
background-position	[[*length*	*percentage*	**left**	**center**	**right**]	[*length*	*percentage*	**top**	**center**	**bottom**]	[**left**	**center**	**right**] || **top**	**center**	**bottom**]]	**inherit**	0% 0%
background-repeat	**repeat**	**repeat-x**	**repeat-y**	**no-repeat**	**inherit**	repeat
border-collapse (applies to table and inline-table elements)	**collapse**	**separate**	**inherit** ^Inherited	separate
border-spacing (applies to table and inline-table elements)	*length length* ?	**inherit** ^Inherited	0

Name	Values	Initial Value
border	[*border-width* || *border-style* || *border-color*] | **inherit**	see individual properties
border-top border-right border-bottom border-left	[*border-width* || *border-style* || *border-color*] | **inherit**	see individual properties
border-color	[*color* | **transparent**] { 1, 4 } | **inherit**	see individual properties
border-top-color border-right-color border-bottom-color border-left-color	*color* | **transparent** | **inherit**	the *color* value of that element
border-style	[**none** | **hidden** | **dotted** | **dashed** | **solid** | **double** | **groove** | **ridge** | **inset** | **outset**] { 1, 4 } | **inherit**	see individual properties
border-top-style border-right-style border-bottom-style border-left-style	[**none** | **hidden** | **dotted** | **dashed** | **solid** | **double** | **groove** | **ridge** | **inset** | **outset**] | **inherit**	none
border-width	[**thin** | **medium** | **thick** | *length*] { 1, 4 } | **inherit**	see individual properties
border-top-width border-right-width border-bottom-width border-left	**thin** | **medium** | **thick** | *length* | **inherit**	medium
bottom (applies to positioned elements)	*length* | *percentage* | **auto** | **inherit**	auto
caption-side (applies to table caption elements)	**top** | **bottom** | **inherit**	top
clear (applies to block-level elements)	**left** | **right** | **both** | **none** | **inherit**	none

175

Name	Values	Initial Value
clip (applies to absolutely positioned elements)	rect(*top* , *right* , *bottom* , *left*) | **auto** | **inherit**	**auto**
color	*color* | **inherit** ^ Inherited	specified by user-agent
content (applies to **:before** and **:after** pseudo elements)	[*string* | *url* | *counter* | **attr(** *identifier*) | **open-quote** | **close-quote** | **no-open-quote** | **no-close-quote**]+ | **normal** | **inherit**	**normal**
counter-increment	[*identifier-integer ?*]+ | **none** | **inherit**	**none**
counter-reset	[*identifier-integer ?*]+ | **none** | **inherit**	**none**
cursor	[[*url* ,]* | **auto** | **default** | **pointer** | **crosshair** | **move** | **e-resize** | **w-resize** | **n-resize** | **ne-resize** | **nw-resize** | **s-resize** | **se-resize** | **sw-resize** | **text** | **wait** | **help** | **progress**] | **inherit** ^ Inherited	**auto**
direction	**ltr** | **rtl** | **inherit** ^ Inherited	**ltr**
display	**none** | **inline** | **block** | **inline-block** | **list-item** | **run-in** | **table** | **inline-table** | **table-row-group** | **table-header-group** | **table-footer-group** | **table-row** | **table-column-group** | **table-column** | **table-cell** | **table-caption** | **inherit**	**inline**
empty-cells (applies to table cell elements)	**show** | **hide** | **inherit** ^ Inherited	**show**
float	**left** | **right** | **none** | **inherit**	**none**

Name	Values	Initial Value
font (may include optional values marked ?)	[[*font-style* || *font-variant* || *font-weight*]? *font-size* [/ *line-height*]? | *font-family*] | **caption** | **icon** | **menu** | **message-box** | **small-caption** | **status-bar** | **inherit** ^ Inherited	see individual properties
font-family (may include optional values marked ?)	[[*family-name* | *generic-family*] ,]* [*family-name* | *generic-family*] | **inherit** ^ Inherited	specified by user-agent
font-size	**xx-small** | **x-small** | **small** | **medium** | **large** | **x-large** | **xx-large** | **smaller** | **larger** | *length* | *percentage* | **inherit** ^ Inherited	medium
font-style	**italic** | **oblique** | **normal** | **inherit** ^ Inherited	normal
font-variant	**small-caps** | **normal** | **inherit** ^ Inherited	normal
font-weight	**normal** | **bold** | **bolder** | **lighter** | **inherit** | **100** | **200** | **300** | **400** | **500** | **600** | **700** | **800** | **900** ^ Inherited	normal
height (applies to block-level and replaced elements)	*length* | *percentage* | **auto** | **inherit**	auto
left (applies to positioned elements)	*length* | *percentage* | **auto** | **inherit**	auto
letter-spacing	*length* | **normal** | **inherit** ^ Inherited	normal
line-height	*length* | *percentage* | *number* | **normal** | **inherit** ^ Inherited	normal

Name	Values	Initial Value
list-style (applies to elements whose display property has a **list-item** value)	[*list-style-type* || *list-style-image* || *list-style-position*] | **inherit** ^ Inherited	see individual properties
list-style-image (applies to elements whose display property has a **list-item** value)	*url* | **none** | **inherit** ^ Inherited	**none**
list-style-position (applies to elements whose display property has a **list-item** value)	**inside** | **outside** | **inherit** ^ Inherited	**outside**
list-style-type (applies to elements whose display property has a **list-item** value)	**disc** | **circle** | **square** | **decimal** | **decimal-leading-zero** | **lower-roman** | **upper-roman** | **lower-greek** | **lower-latin** | **upper-latin** | **armenian** | **georgian** | **none** | **inherit** ^ Inherited	**disc**
margin	[*length* | *percentage* | **auto**] { 1 , 4 } | **inherit**	see individual properties
margin-top **margin-right** **margin-bottom** **margin-left**	*length* | *percentage* | **auto** | **inherit**	0
max-height **max-width** (applies to all elements except inline non-replaced elements and table elements)	*length* | *percentage* | **none** | **inherit**	**none**
min-height **min-width** (applies to all elements except inline non-replaced elements and table elements)	*length* | *percentage* | **inherit**	0

Name	Values	Initial Value
outline	[*outline-color* || *outline-style* || *outline-width*] | inherit	see individual properties
outline-color	*color* | **invert** | **inherit**	invert
outline-style	**none** | **dotted** | **dashed** | **solid** | **double** | **groove** | **ridge** | **inset** | **outset** | **inherit**	none
outline-width	**thin** | **medium** | **thick** | *length* | **inherit**	medium
overflow (applies to block-level and replaced elements)	**visible** | **hidden** | **scroll** | **auto** | **inherit**	visible
padding	[*length* | *percentage*] { 1 , 4 } | **inherit**	see individual properties
padding-top padding-right padding-bottom padding-left	*length* | *percentage* | **inherit**	0
position	**static** | **relative** | **absolute** | **fixed** | **inherit**	static
quotes	[*string string*]+ | **none** | **inherit**	specified by user-agent
right (applies to positioned elements)	*length* | *percentage* | **auto** | **inherit**	auto
table-layout (applies to table and inline-table elements)	**auto** | **fixed** | **inherit**	auto
text-align (applies to block-level elements)	**left** | **center** | **right** | **justify** | **inherit** ^ Inherited	specified by user-agent
text-decoration	[**underline** || **overline** || **line-through** || **blink**] | **none** | **inherit**	none

Name	Values	Initial Value
text-indent (applies to block-level elements)	*length* | *percentage* | **inherit** ^ Inherited	0
text-transform	**uppercase** | **lowercase** | **capitalize** | **none** | **inherit** ^ Inherited	none
top (applies to positioned elements)	*length* | *percentage* | **auto** | **inherit**	auto
unicode-bidi	**normal** | **embed** | **bidi-override** | **inherit**	normal
vertical-align (applies to inline elements and table cells)	**baseline** | **sub** | **super** | **top** | **middle** | **bottom** | **text-top** | **text-bottom** | *length* | *percentage* | **inherit**	baseline
visibility	**visible** | **hidden** | **collapse** | **inherit** ^ Inherited	inherit
white-space	**normal** | **nowrap** | **pre** | **pre-wrap** | **pre-line** | **inherit** ^ Inherited	normal
width (applies to block-level and replaced elements)	*length* | *percentage* | **auto** | **inherit**	auto
word-spacing	**normal** | *length* | **inherit** ^ Inherited	normal
z-index (applies to positioned elements)	**auto** | *integer* | **inherit**	auto

Selectors

The following tables in this section provide a brief description of each type of CSS selector together with its syntax pattern and an example style rule using that selector:

Universal selector

Matches any element in the HTML document.
If a rule has no explicit selector the universal selector is inferred

Pattern:	*
Example: Select all elements	* { color: green }

Element selector

Matches the specified named element in the HTML document.
Every instance of the named element is matched

Pattern:	element
Example: Select all **<p>** paragraph elements	p { color: green }

Descendant selector

Matches a specified element that is a descendant of another specified element.
The matched element can be of any descendant level – child, grandchild, etc.

Pattern:	element descendant-element
Example: Select all **<li>** list item elements of both ordered and unordered lists contained within any **<div>** element (child descendants of **<ol>** and **<ul>** elements – grandchildren of **<div>**)	div li { color: green }

Child selector

Matches a specified element that is a child of another specified element. This is more precise than the descendant selector as it only matches direct child elements

Pattern: element > child-element

Example:
Select each **\<p>** paragraph element that is a   **div > p { color: green }**
direct child of a **\<div>** element

Adjacent sibling selector

Matches an element that immediately follows a specified sibling element in the document tree relationship

Pattern: element + sibling-element

Example:
Select each **\<p>** paragraph element that   **h3 + p { color: green }**
immediately follows any **\<h3>** element

Class selector

Matches the name assigned to a "class" attribute of an element using dot notation

Pattern: element class-name

Example:
Select each **\<p>** paragraph element with a   **p.grn { color: green }**
class attribute value of "grn"

ID selector

Matches the name assigned to an "id" attribute of an element using hash notation

Pattern: element #id-name

Example:
Select each **\<p>** paragraph element with an   **p#grn { color: green }**
id attribute value of "grn"

Attribute selector

Matches any element that includes the specified attribute

Pattern: element[attribute]

Example:
Select each **<a>** anchor element that has an   **a[href] { color: green }**
href attribute, regardless of its value

Attribute value selector

Matches the exact value assigned to a specified attribute to select that element

Pattern: element[attribute = "value"]

Example:
Select each **<a>** anchor element with an   **a[href = "home"] { color: green }**
exact **href** attribute value of "home"

Listed attribute value selector

Matches the exact value from a space-separated list of values assigned to a specified
attribute to select that element

Pattern: element[attribute ~= "value"]

Example:
Select each **<span>** element that includes a   **span[class~="grn"] {color: green}**
class attribute value of "grn"

Partial attribute value selector

Matches the first part of a hyphenated value assigned to a specified attribute to select
that element

Pattern: element[attribute |= "value"]

Example:
Select each **<span>** element containing a
hyphenated **lang** attribute value beginning   **span[lang |="es"] { color: green }**
with "es"

Pseudo-classes

The following tables in this section list each CSS pseudo-class together with a description of its application and an example style rule using that pseudo-class:

:lang()

Applies to an element based on the human language encoding as defined in the document header or by a **lang** attribute value. Works like the **|=** partial attribute value selector matching both single and hyphenated language identifiers (like "es" and "es-mx")

Example:
Select each **<span>** element defined as Spanish language encoding

span:lang(es) { color: green }

:first-child

Applies to any element that is the first child of another element in the document tree relationship – the specified element is itself the target, not the first child of that element

Example:
Select each **<span>** element that is itself the first child of an outer containing element

span:first-child { color: green }

:focus

Applies to an element during the time when it has the interface focus to accept keyboard events. Easiest recognized when an HTML form input box is displaying the text-input cursor – ready for the user to input text

Example:
Select each **<input>** element when it has the interface focus ready to receive text input

input:focus { background: lime }

:link

Applies to a hyperlink that is not known to have been visited according to the user-agent's history – the "link" state is mutually exclusive with the "visited" state described in the next table below

Example:
Select each **<a>** anchor element with an unvisited hyperlink status

a:link { color: green }

:visited

Applies to a hyperlink that is known to have been visited according to the user agent's history – the "visited" state is mutually exclusive with the "link" state described in the previous table above

Example:
Select each **<a>** anchor element with a visited hyperlink status

a:visited { color: red }

:hover

Applies to an element during the time when it is designated without being activated – hovering the mouse pointer within its boundaries to fire the "mouseover" interface event

Example:
Select each **<span>** element when it is designated by the mouse pointer hovering over it

span:hover { background: lime }

:active

Applies to an element during the time when it is activated – clicking the mouse button within its boundaries to fire the "mousedown" interface event

Example:
Select each **<span>** element when it is activated by the mouse button clicking on it

span:active { background: red }

Pseudo-elements

The following tables in this section list each CSS pseudo-element together with a description of what it generates and an example style rule using that pseudo-element:

:before

Generates a pseudo-element to insert content before all other content in the specified HTML element

Example:	
Select each **\<p\>** paragraph element and insert an opening square bracket before all other content	**p:before { content: "[" }**

:after

Generates a pseudo-element to insert content after all other content in the specified HTML element

Example:	
Select each **\<p\>** paragraph element and insert a closing square bracket after all other content	**p:after { content: "]" }**

:first-letter

Generates a pseudo-element to style the very first letter of text contained within a specified element

Example:	
Select the first letter within each **\<p\>** paragraph element	**p:first-letter { font-size: larger }**

:first-line

Generates a pseudo-element to style the very first line of text contained within a specified element

Example:	
Select the first line within each **\<p\>** paragraph element	**p:first-line { color: green }**